# Stamford Sketchb

*by Karen Neale*

To Mike and Jackie
with best wishes
Karen Neale

Published by
Walker's Books Limited

For my son Gabriel with love.
To my husband Alex, and my mum and dad with love
and thanks for all your help and support.
Thank you also to our new friends for a warm welcome
to Stamford!

Published by
Walker's Books Limited, Oakham, Rutland. U.K. LE15 6AH

ISBN 9780955119729
First published 2011



Designed by Philip Walker

Printed in Great Britain by Pegasus Colourprint Limited. CR4 4NF

# Contents

# INTRODUCTION

Stamford is a special place. The town and its people are friendly and welcoming. It is an untarnished treasure, discovered by the discerning, and for me, it feels like I've come home. I moved to Stamford with my young family in autumn 2010. I've known about Stamford's appeal for a long time as I grew up in Spalding, not far from Stamford and my parents still live locally.

My passion is sketching and painting the world around me in my annotated, sketchbook diaries. So it was not long after my arrival that I was out and about in Stamford with my sketchbook. I stand 'in situ' and draw with an ordinary black biro as much as I can of what is going on around me in my book. Then, I add colour with my small field box of watercolours. The notes I make around the perimeter are observations I've made whilst I've been sketching. It is a great privilege and pleasure to simply spend time in a place and draw, and it is a wonderful way to get to know a place and in this case Stamford.

I've kept sketchbooks since leaving school, throughout my architectural studies at Newcastle and Sheffield Universities, subsequent move to London and eventual qualification as an architect in 1999. My sketchbooks have taken me on some wonderful adventures. In 2001, I was awarded a Churchill Fellowship to undertake an artist's journey through World Heritage Cities and Sites from France, travelling eastwards through eight countries to Nepal, recording it all in my sketchbook diary. Subsequently I spent time in Cuba, culminating with a solo exhibition of my work at the British Ambassador's Residence in Havana.

Closer to home, I continued the World Heritage theme with a community project along Hadrian's Wall. Then in London, I was privileged to sketch in and around the Palace of Westminster and was artist in residence at the Athenaeum Club in 2004. Rather auspiciously I was appointed 'MCC Young Cricket Artist for 2005', based at Lord's Cricket Ground, and subsequently artist in residence at The Queen's Club for the 2007 tennis season.

I've had some fabulous commissions. In 2006, The Winston Churchill Memorial Trust commissioned me to produce a painting to present to Her Majesty the Queen. I've also worked with Bob Wilson's charity, The Willow Foundation, sketching in and around Arsenal's football stadiums.

In October 2006, my first London sketchbook diary was published by Methuen, entitled 'London in Landscape' with Winston Churchill's daughter, Lady Soames generously writing the foreword. In 2009, the second volume of 'London in Landscape' was launched with an exhibition of my paintings in the Barbican Centre, London. Now in 2011, Walkers, Stamford's local bookshop, is publishing my Stamford sketchbook.

Stamford's stony streets and buildings are steeped in history and they are also thriving in the 21st century. My sketchbook reflects this, from Barn Hill to Burghley House, and St. Paul's Street to St. Peter's Hill. I hope you will enjoy this book as much as I have in its creation. Further information about 'me and my work' can be found at: www.karenneale.co.uk.

Karen Neale, Stamford, September 2011

# FOREWORD

It is perhaps fitting that the first illustration in this wonderful book, takes as its subject the same view of Stamford as chosen by those famous topographers, Samuel and Nathaniel Buck, on their visit here in 1743.

Since then, there has been a succession of talented artists who have come here to draw and paint the town's panoramas and streets. We've had the delicate sketches of William Twopenny and John Claude Nattes, also the denser pencil drawings of Frederick Griggs, who came here just before the First World War. There was the famous caricaturist, Thomas Rowlandson, who gave us the delightful image of St Mary's Hill in 1822. Then come the watercolourists. Turner, who set up his easel in High Street St Martin's, a few years after Rowlandson, and gave us a vision of Stamford just after a storm - a similar view is presented here. And we cannot forget the talented Wilfrid Wood who gave us many memorable streetscapes from the 1930s until his death in 1976.

What is common to all these artists, is that they were people who came to Stamford and were enthralled by its beauty. I remember coming to Stamford myself in the early eighties and being amazed by this relatively unknown gem of a town. I think the same spirit pervades here. Karen Neale is a newcomer to Stamford and the artist within her has resonated with the special story of this town, a story written in its winding streets and mellow stone buildings.

Karen brings the story right up to date and her wide-screen street scenes and panoramas are full of the bustle and life of this energetic market town. Sketched and painted on the streets themselves, they capture the colours, life, soul and spirit of the place in an immediate and exciting way. As such they are an important contribution to the artistic record of this unique Lincolnshire town.

Martin Smith
Stamford
September 2011

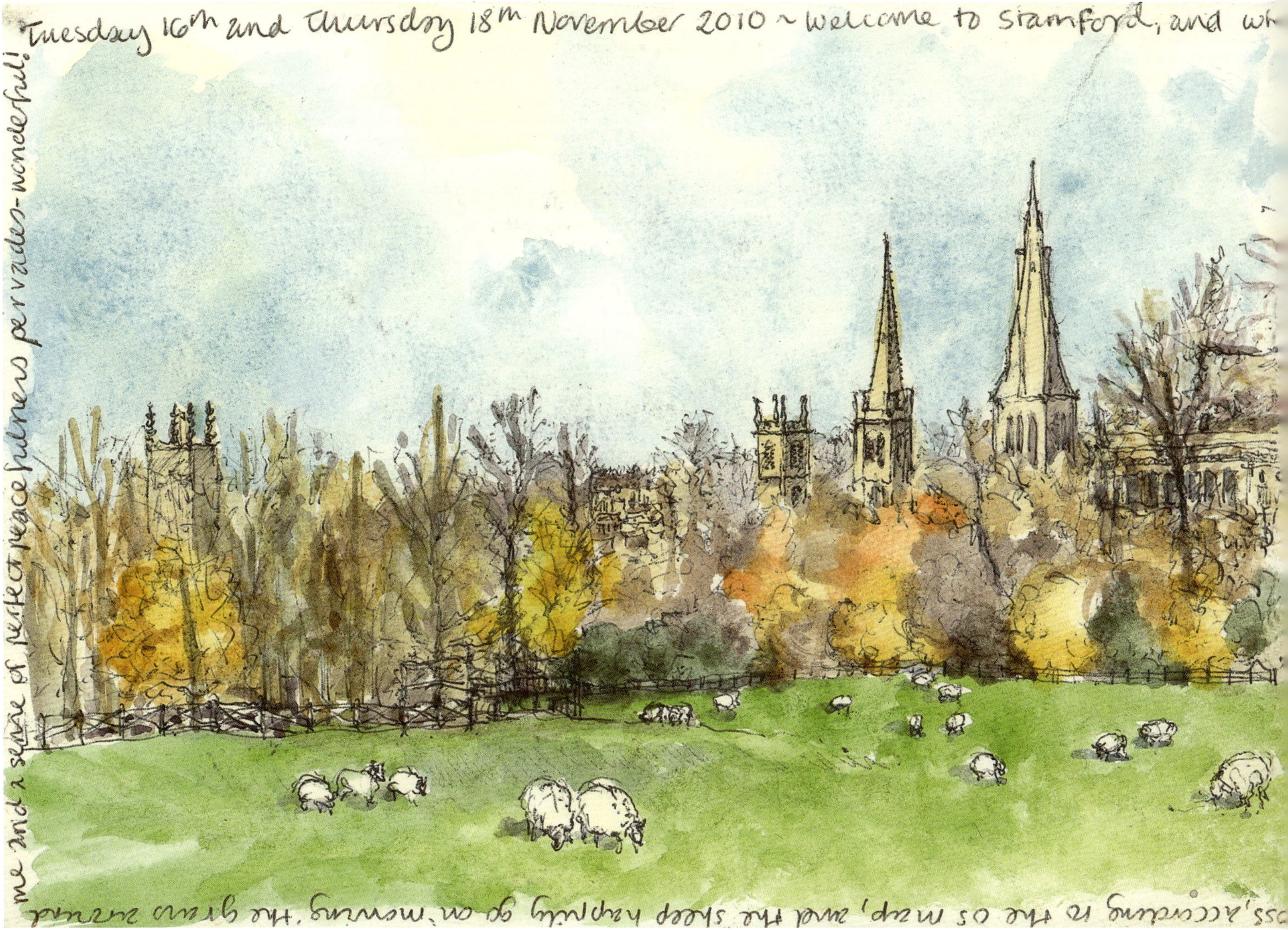
Tuesday 16th and Thursday 18th November 2010 ~ welcome to Stamford, and wh
oss, according to the OS map, and the sheep happily go on 'mowing' the grass around
me and a sense of perfect peacefulness pervades - wonderful!

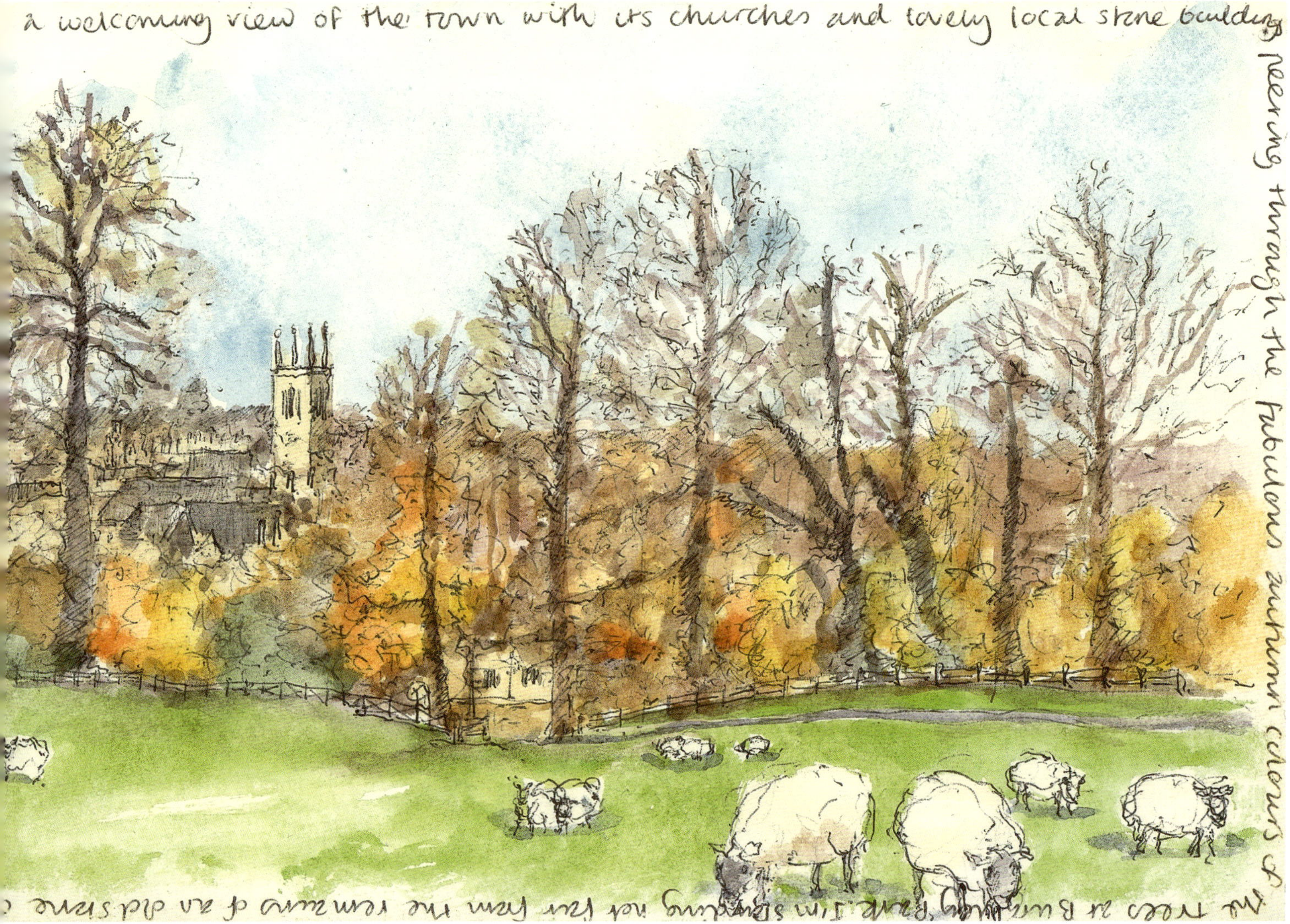
a welcoming view of the town with its churches and lovely local stone building
peering through the fabulous autumn colours of

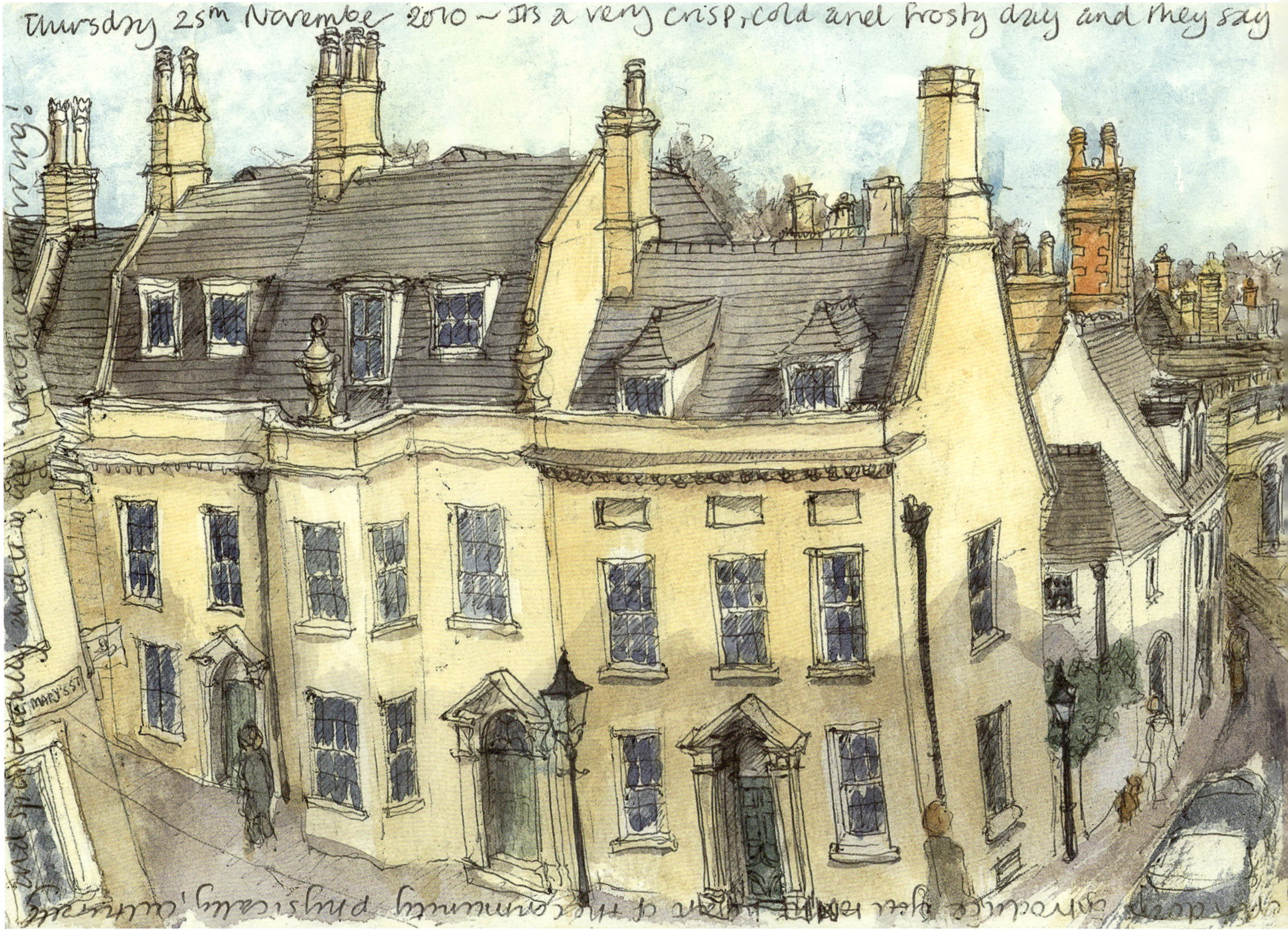
Thursday 25th November 2010 ~ It's a very crisp, cold and frosty day and they say
ST MARY'S ST

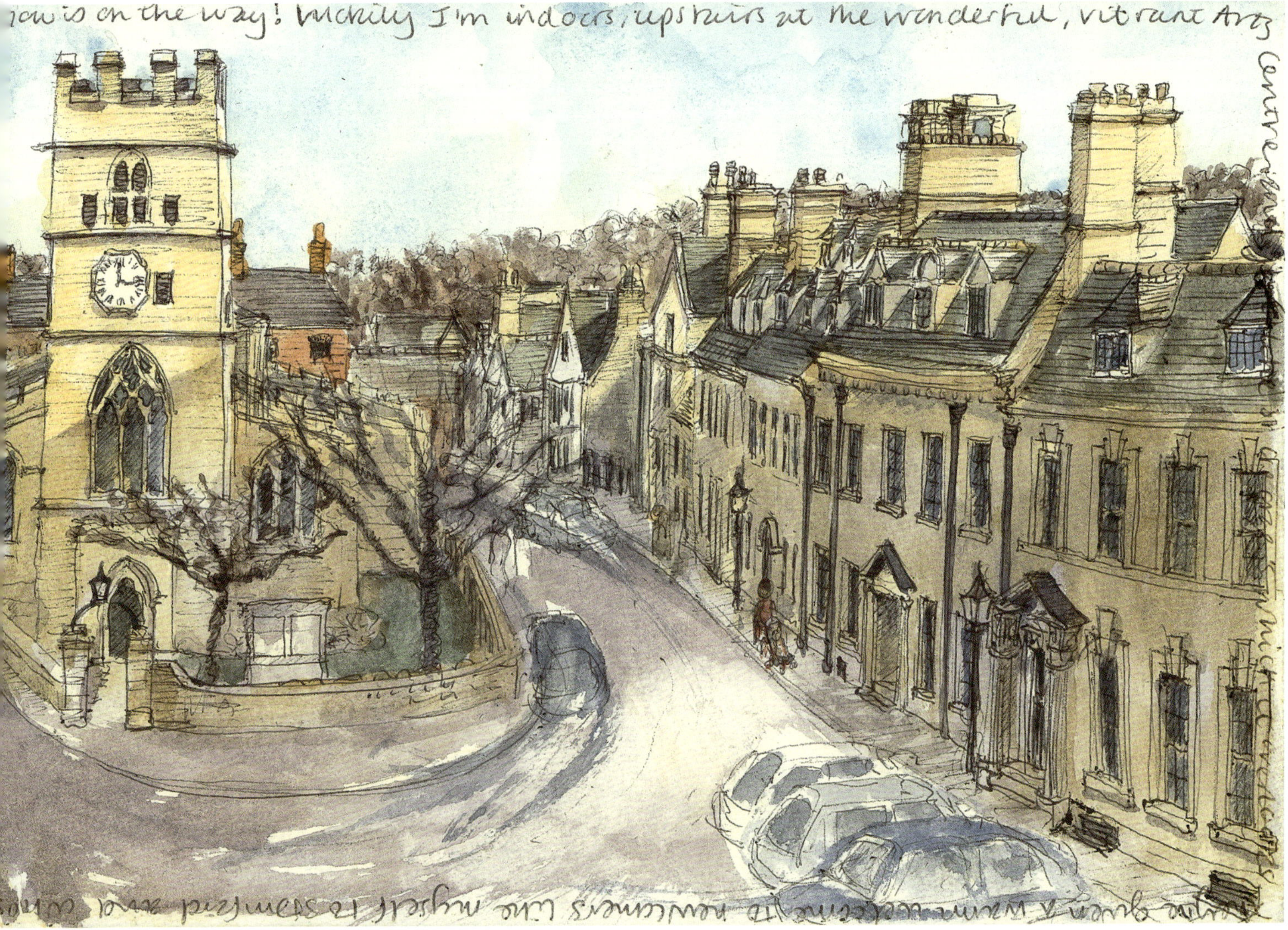
now is on the way! Luckily I'm indoors, upstairs at the wonderful, vibrant Arts
Centre

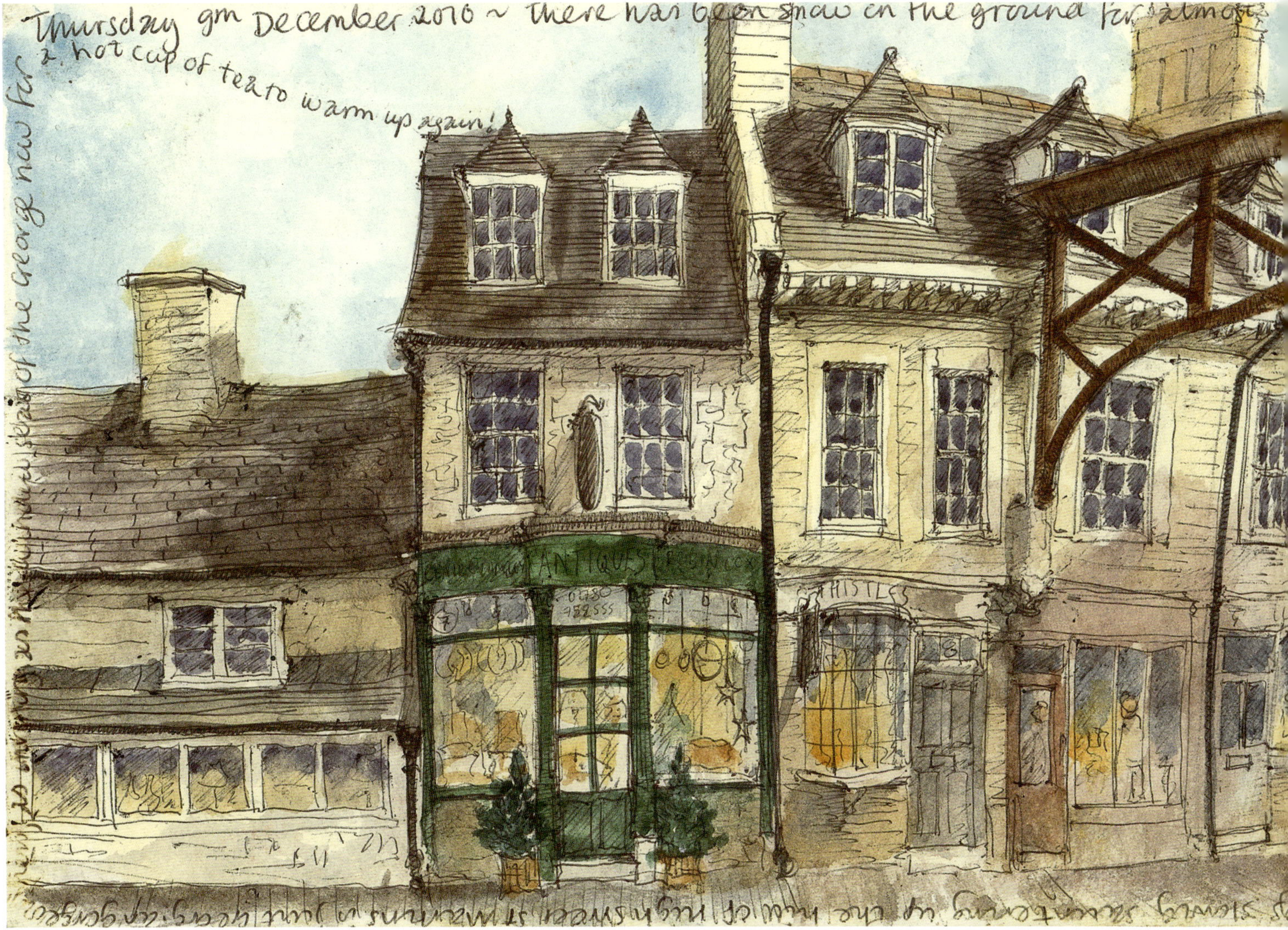

Thursday 9th December 2010 ~ There has been snow on the ground for almost
a hot cup of tea to warm up again!
ANTIQUES

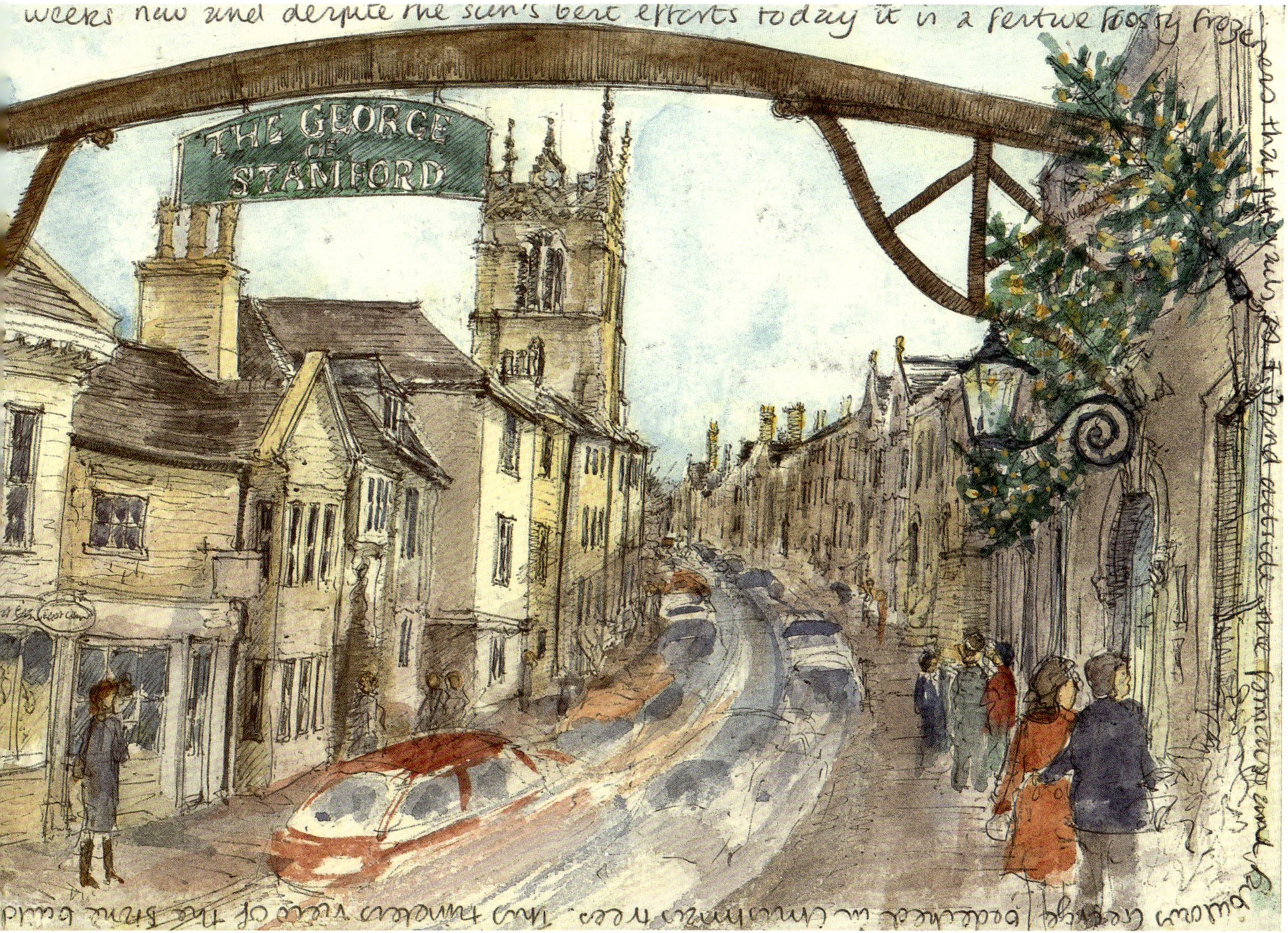
weeks now and despite the sun's best efforts today it is a festive frosty froze
THE GEORGE OF STAMFORD

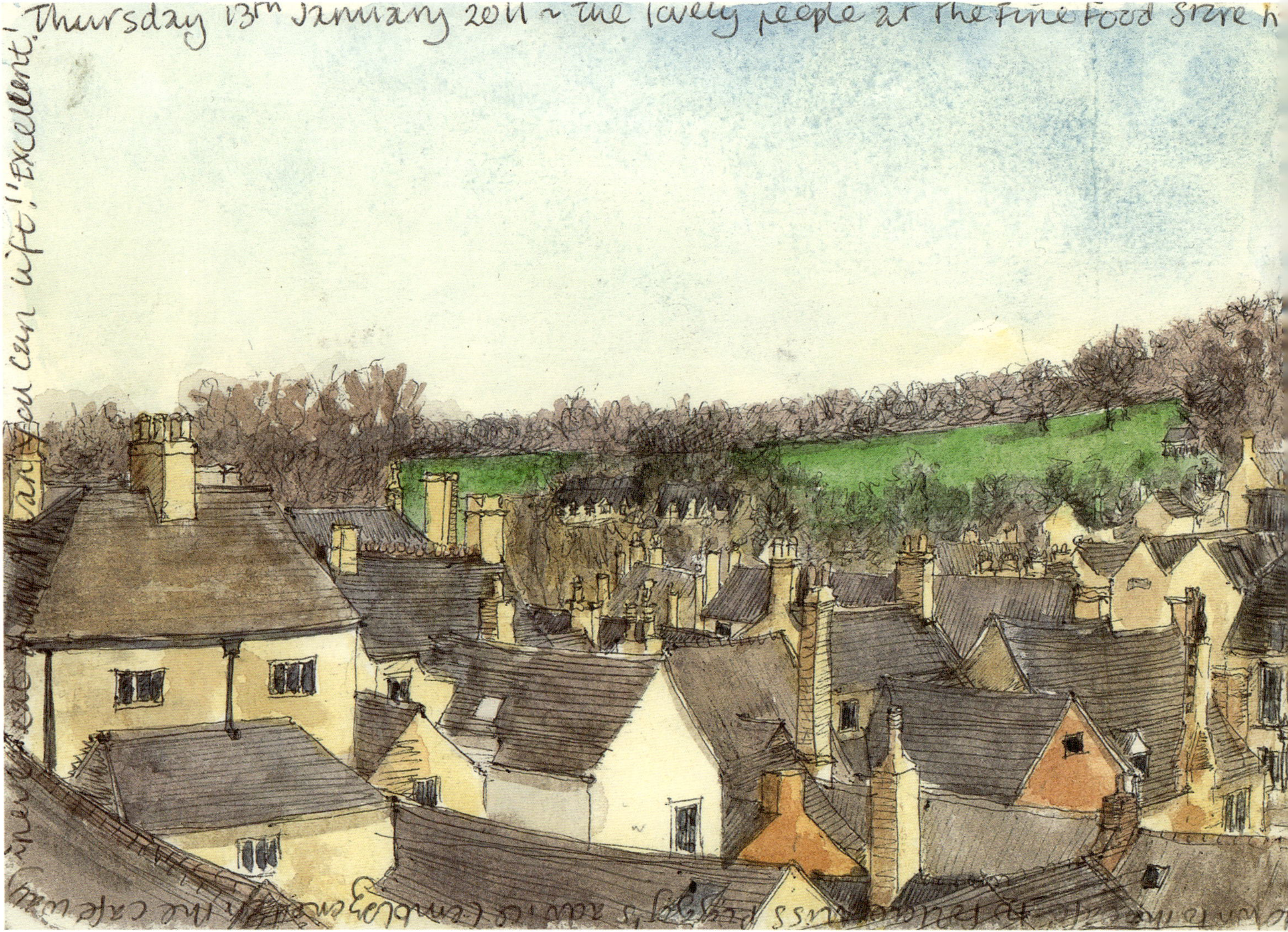
Thursday 13th January 2011 ~ the lovely people at the Fine Food Store
you can lift! 'Excellent!'

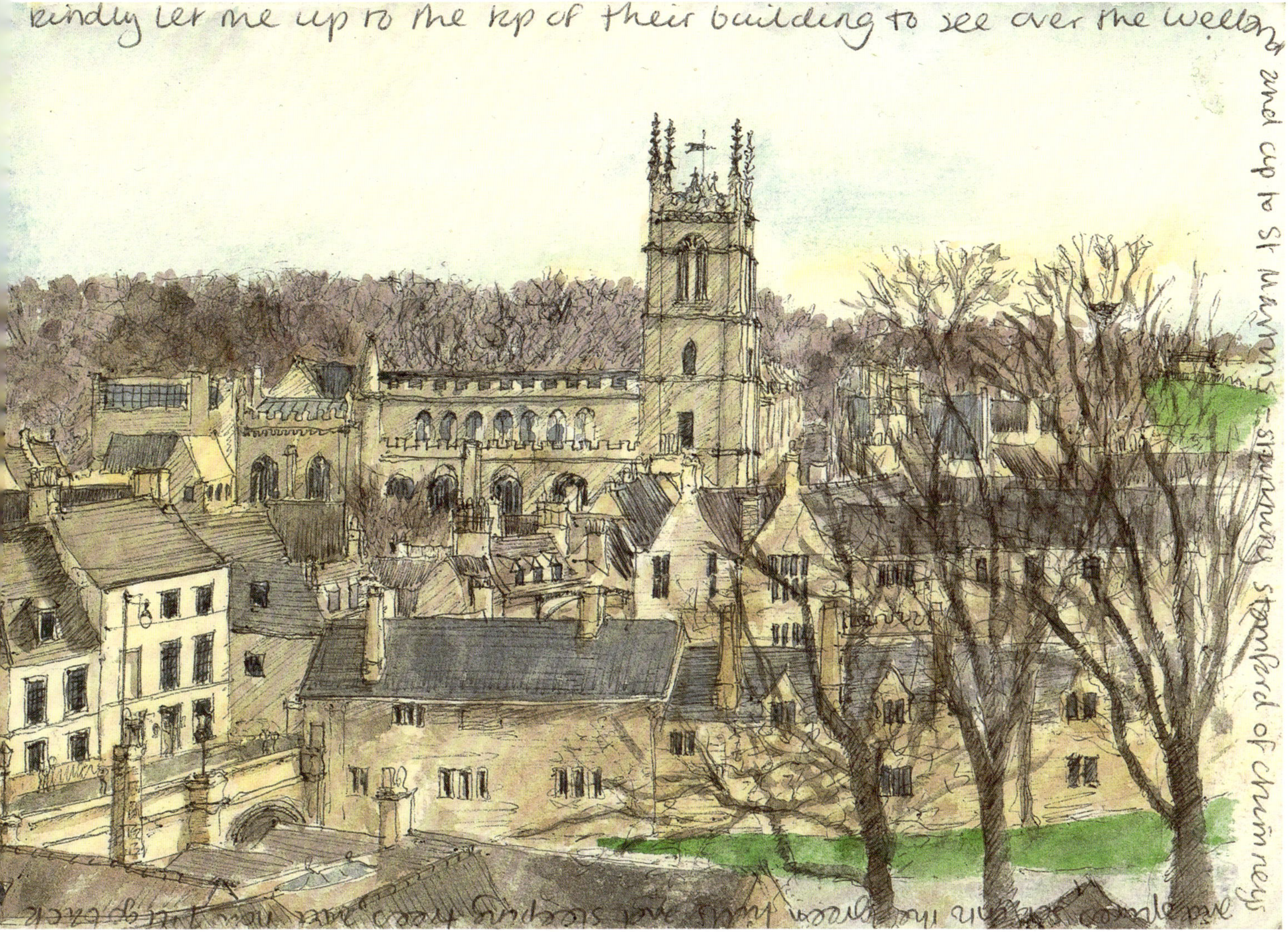
kindly let me up to the top of their building to see over the Welland
and up to St Martins - stunning stamford of chimneys
green hills and sleeping trees and now I'll go back

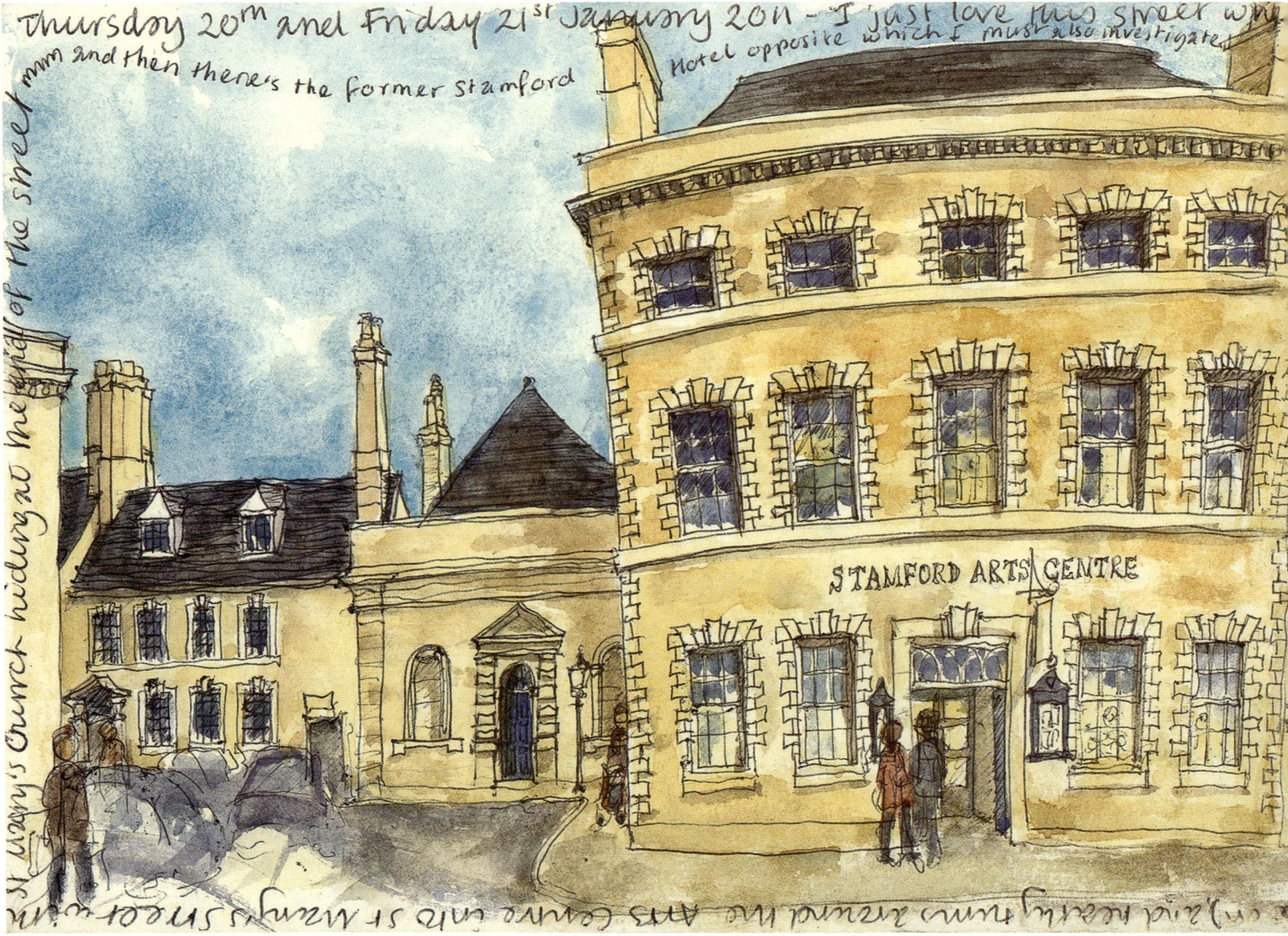
Thursday 20th and Friday 21st January 2011 - I just love this street
mm and then there's the former Stamford Hotel opposite which I must also investigate
St Mary's Church hiding at the end of the street
STAMFORD ARTS CENTRE
and nearly runs around the Arts Centre into St Mary's Street

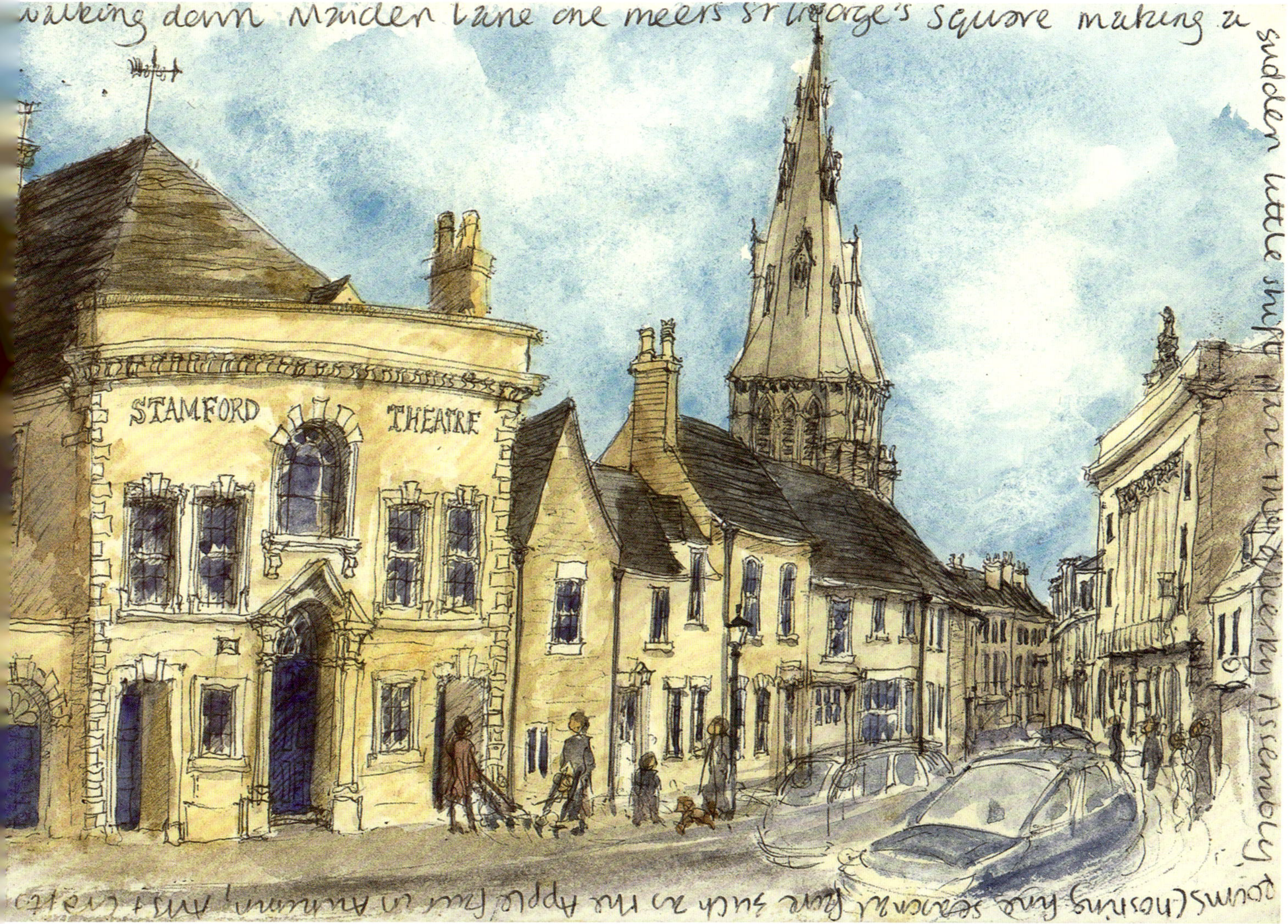
walking down Maiden Lane one meets St George's Square making a
STAMFORD
THEATRE

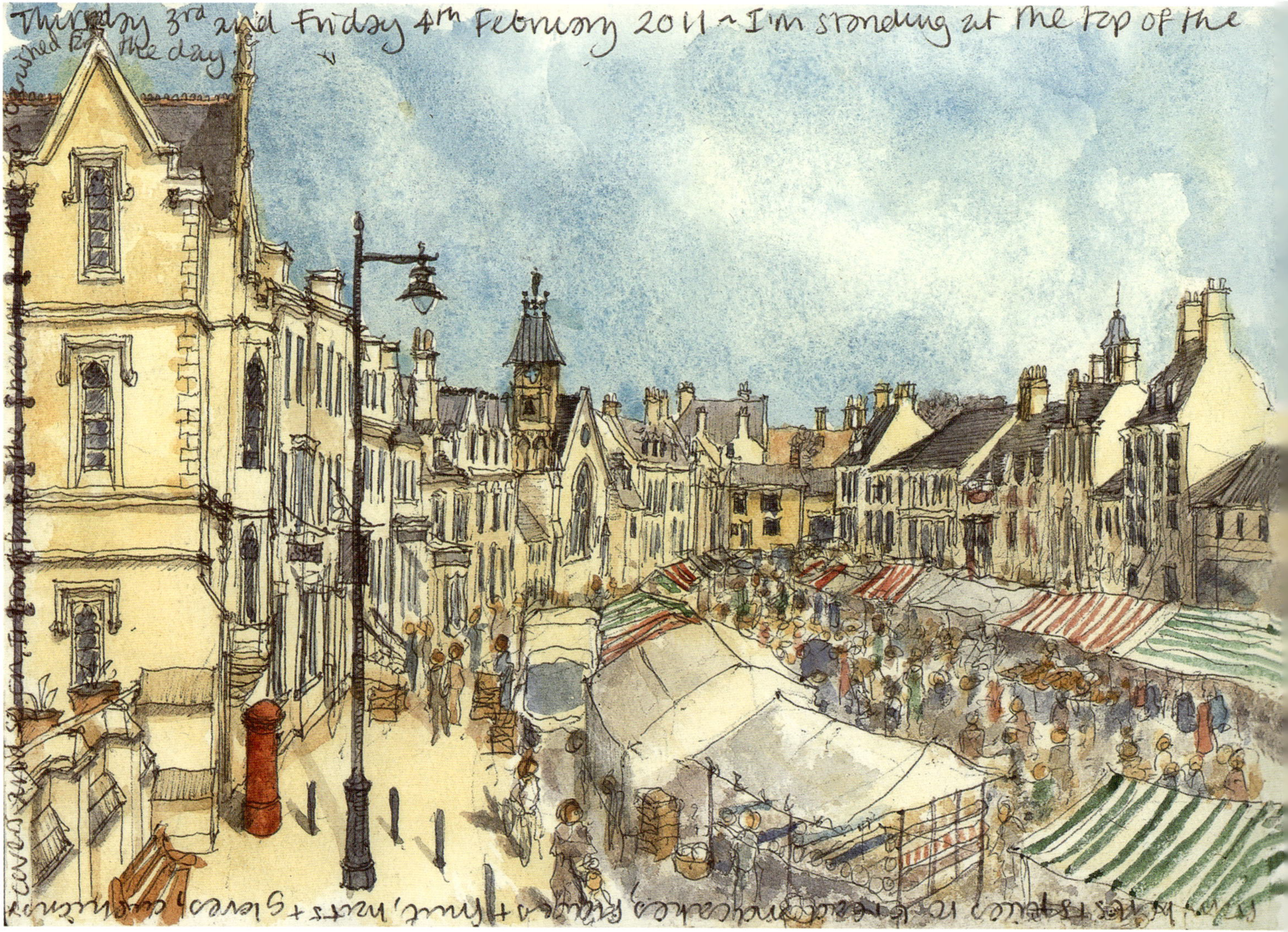
Thursday 3rd and Friday 4th February 2011 ~ I'm standing at the top of the
finished for the day.

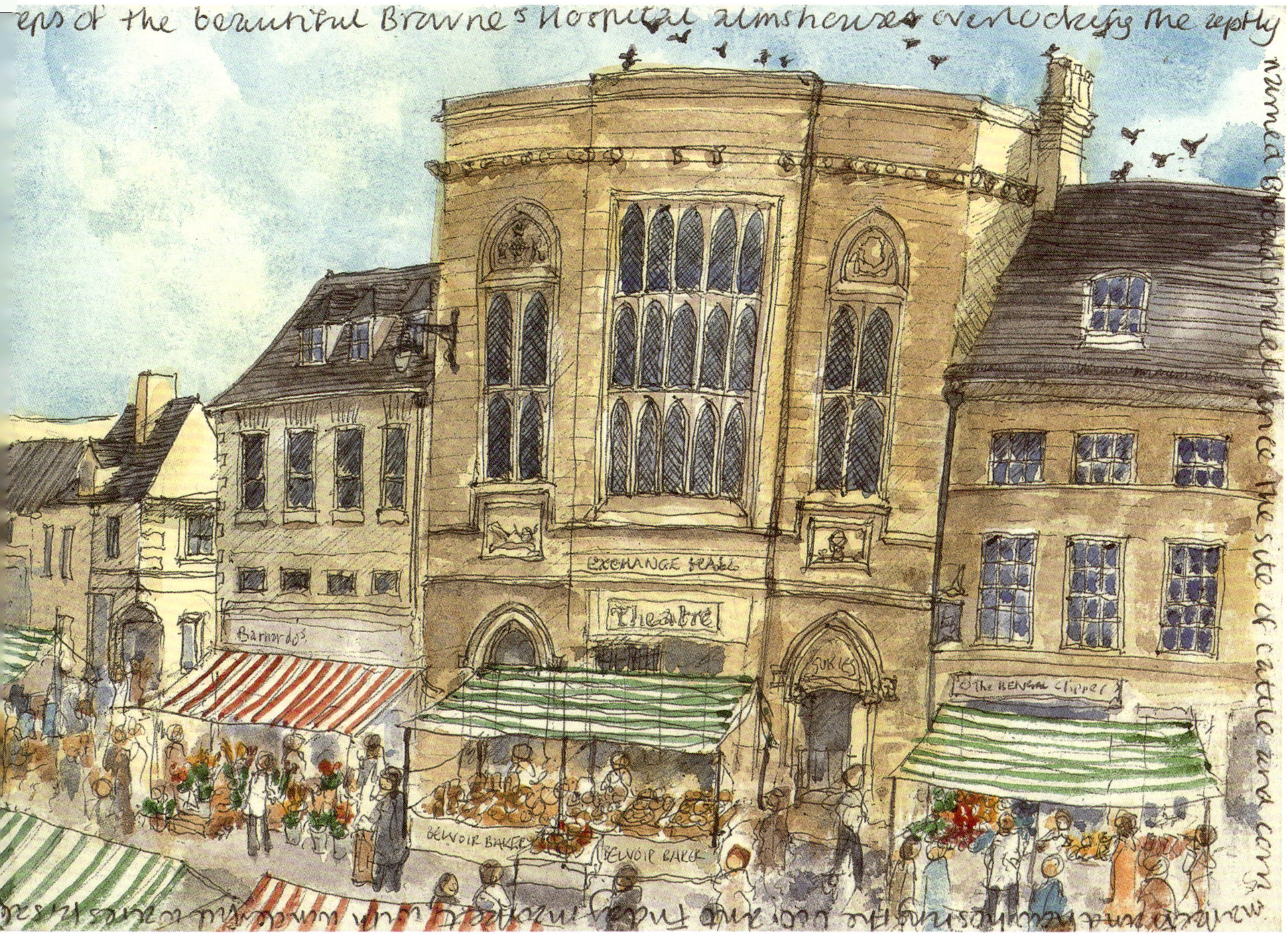
eps of the beautiful Browne's Hospital almshouses overlooking the aptly
named Broad Street once the site of cattle and corn
EXCHANGE HALL
Theatre
Barnardo's
SUKIES
The BENGAL Clipper
BELVOIR BAKER

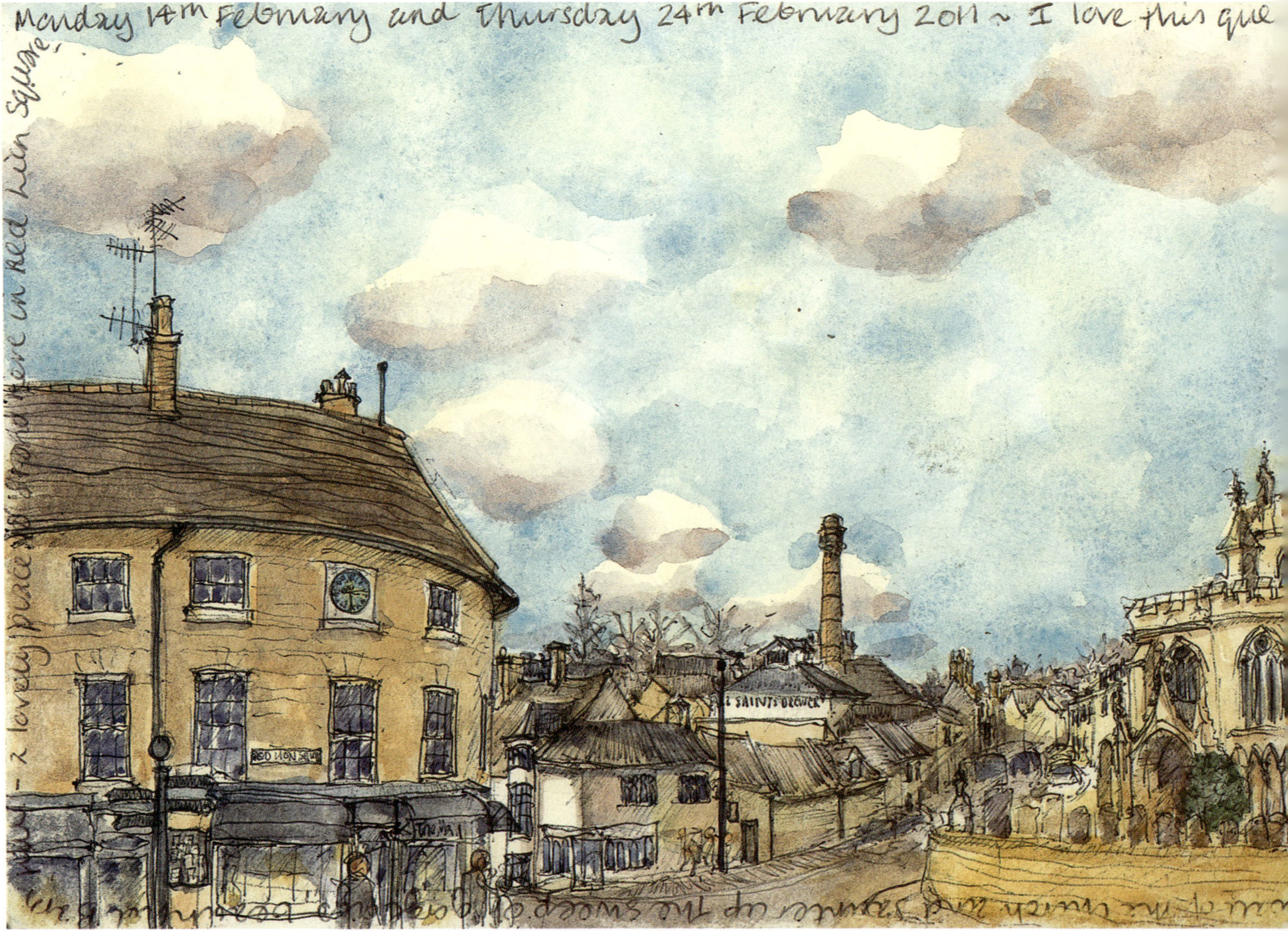
Monday 14th February and Thursday 24th February 2011 ~ I love this que
– a lovely place to stand here in Red Lion Square,
the church and square up the sweep of

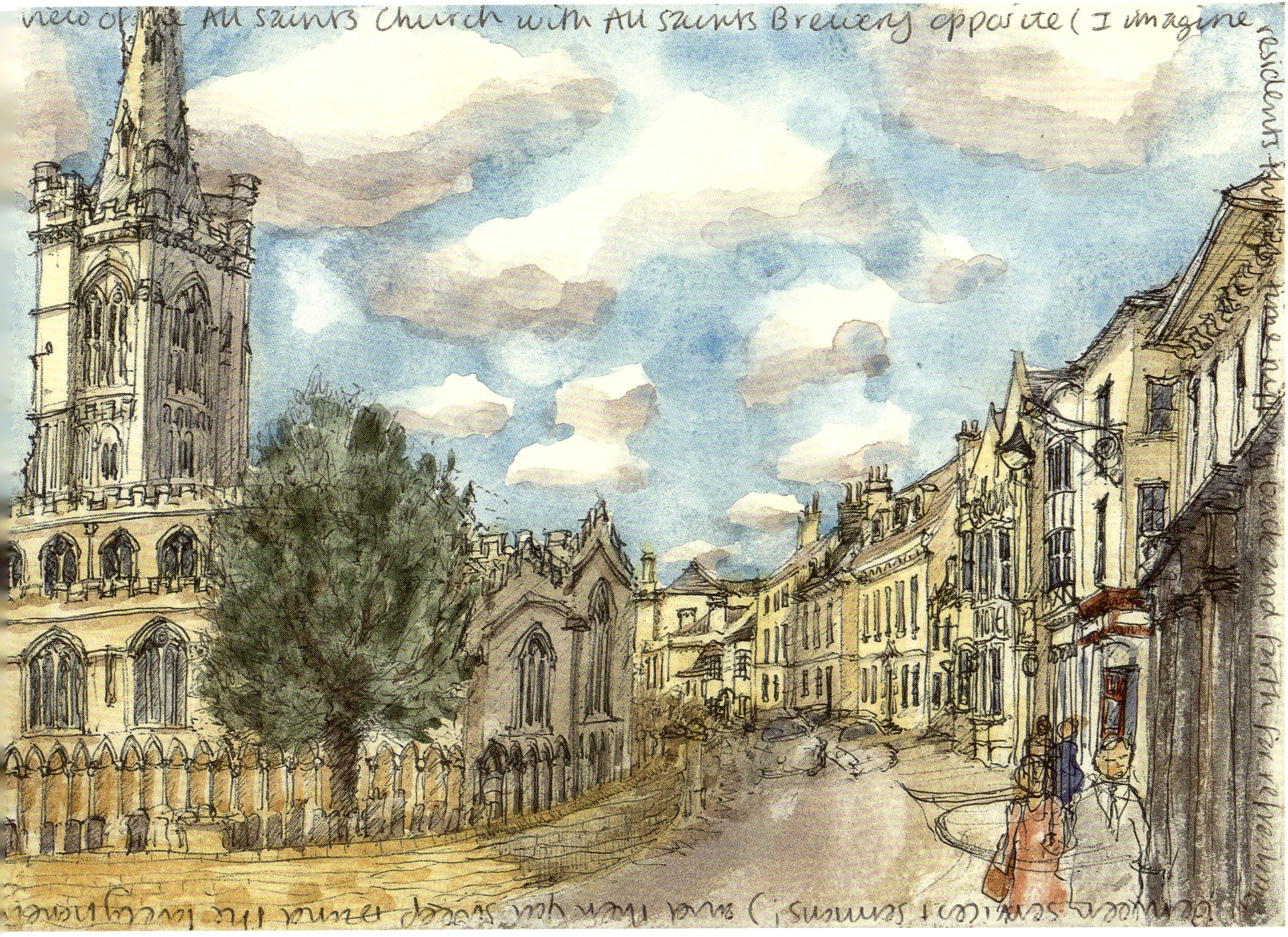
view of the All Saints Church with All Saints Brewery opposite ( I imagine

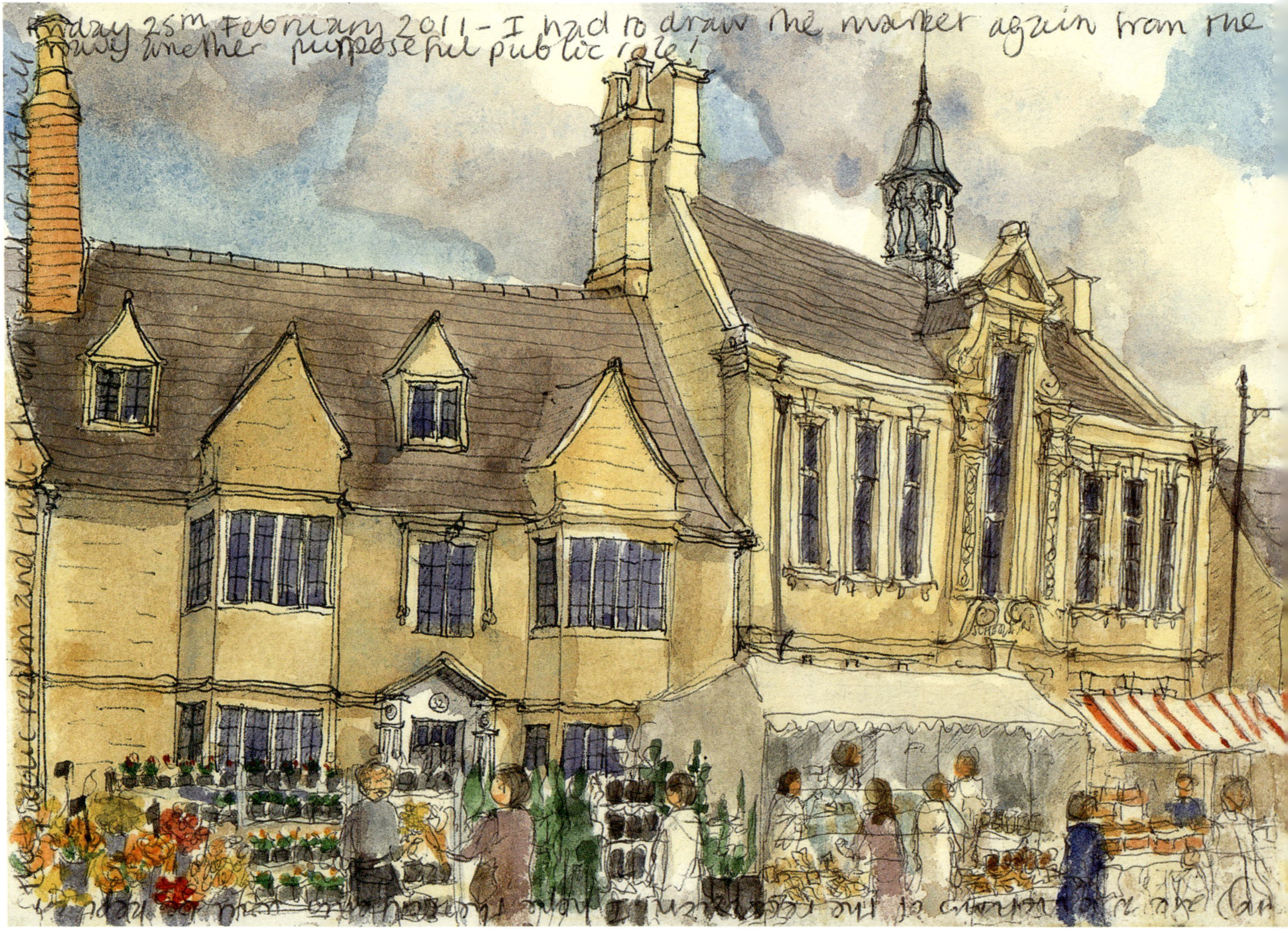
Friday 25th February 2011 – I had to draw the market again from the
another purposeful public role!

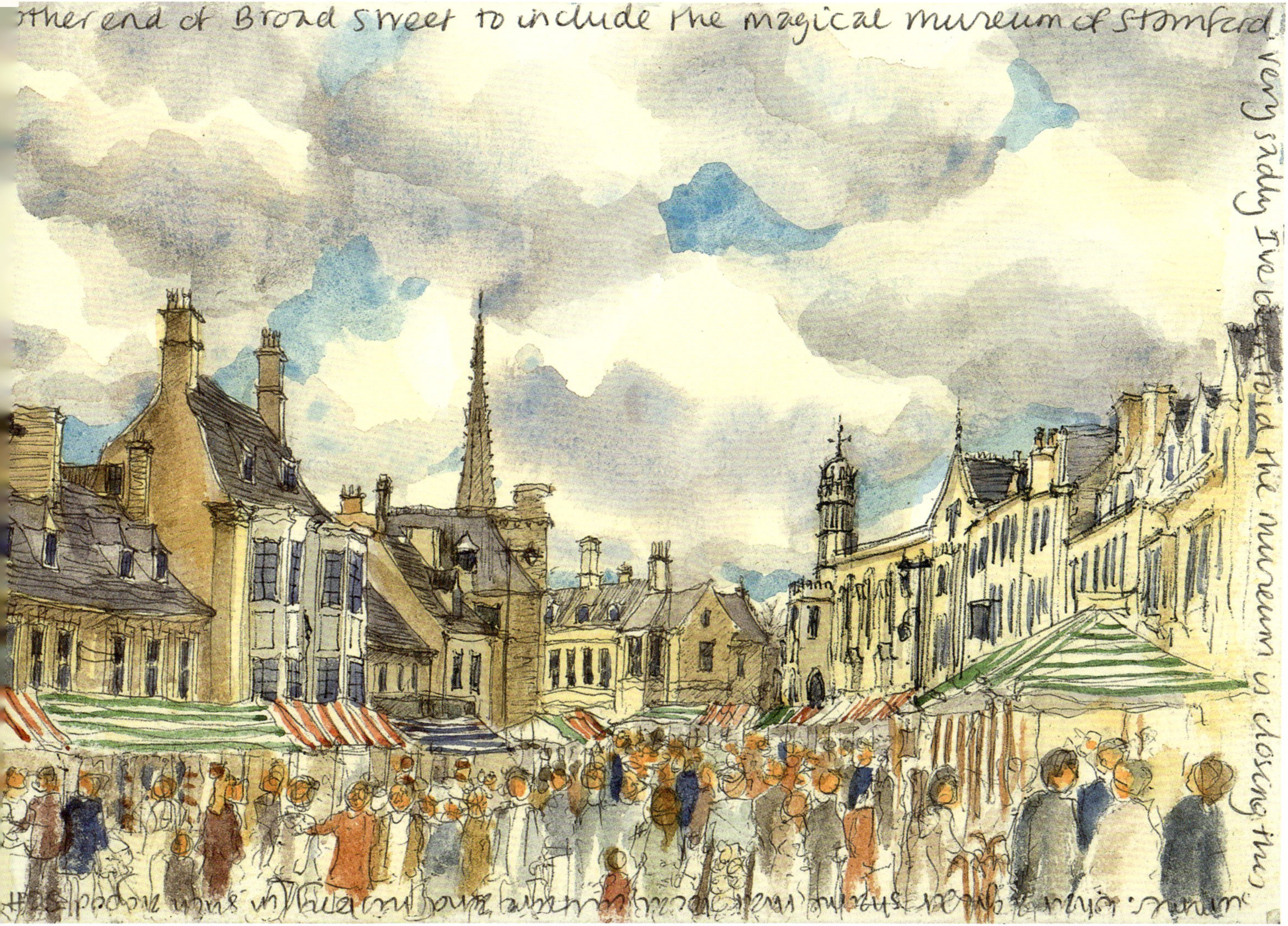
other end of Broad Street to include the magical museum of Stamford
very sadly I've been told the museum is closing this

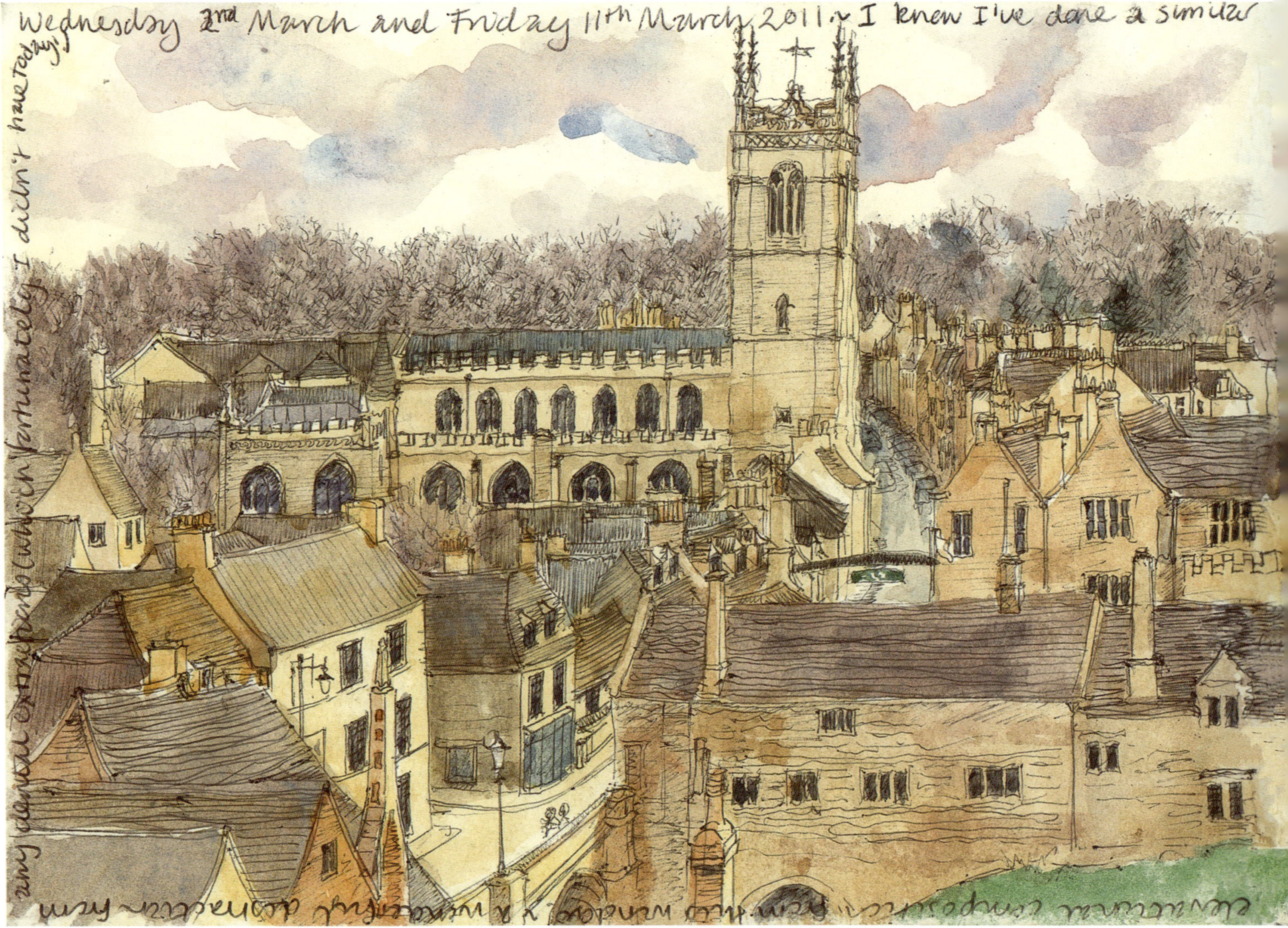
Wednesday 2nd March and Friday 11th March 2011. I knew I've done a similar
elevational composition from this window & a wonderful distraction from
any damned errands (which fortunately I didn't have today!)

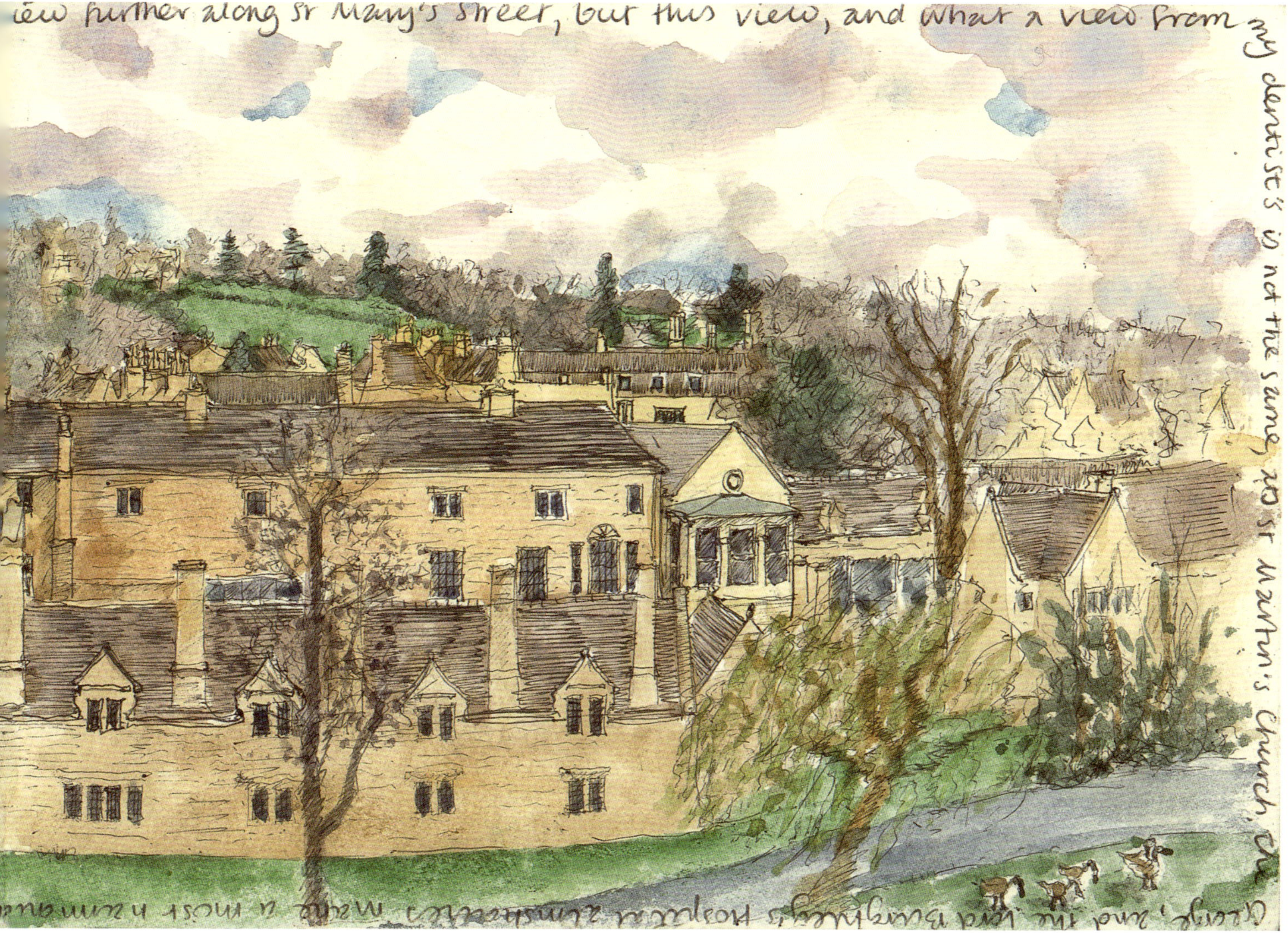
iew further along St Mary's Street, but this view, and what a view from
my dentist's is not the same, to St Martin's Church, St
George, and the Lord Burghley's Hospital almshouses make a most harmonious

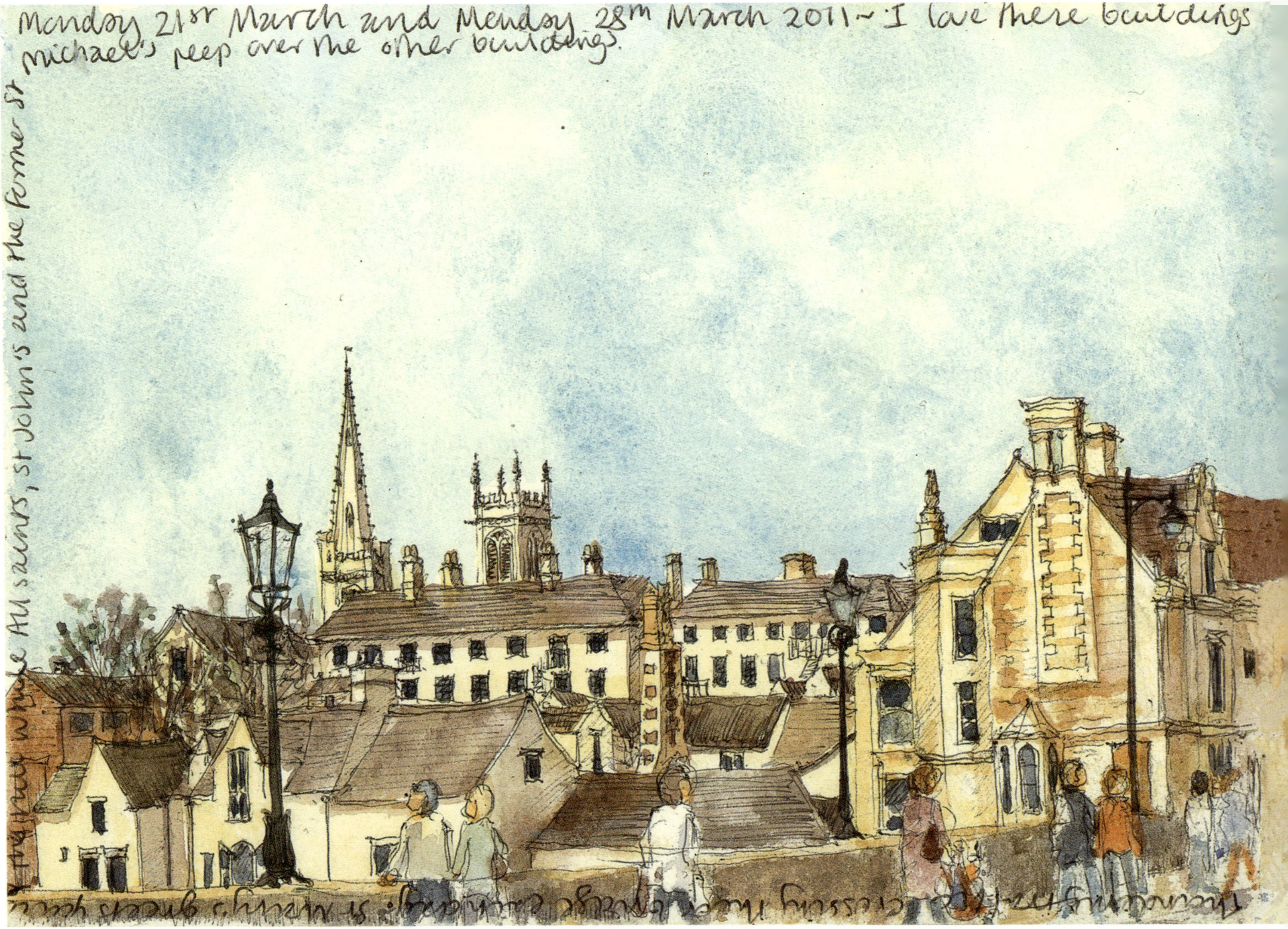
Monday 21st March and Monday 28th March 2011 ~ I love these buildings
the whole All Saints, St John's and the former St
Michael's peep over the other buildings.

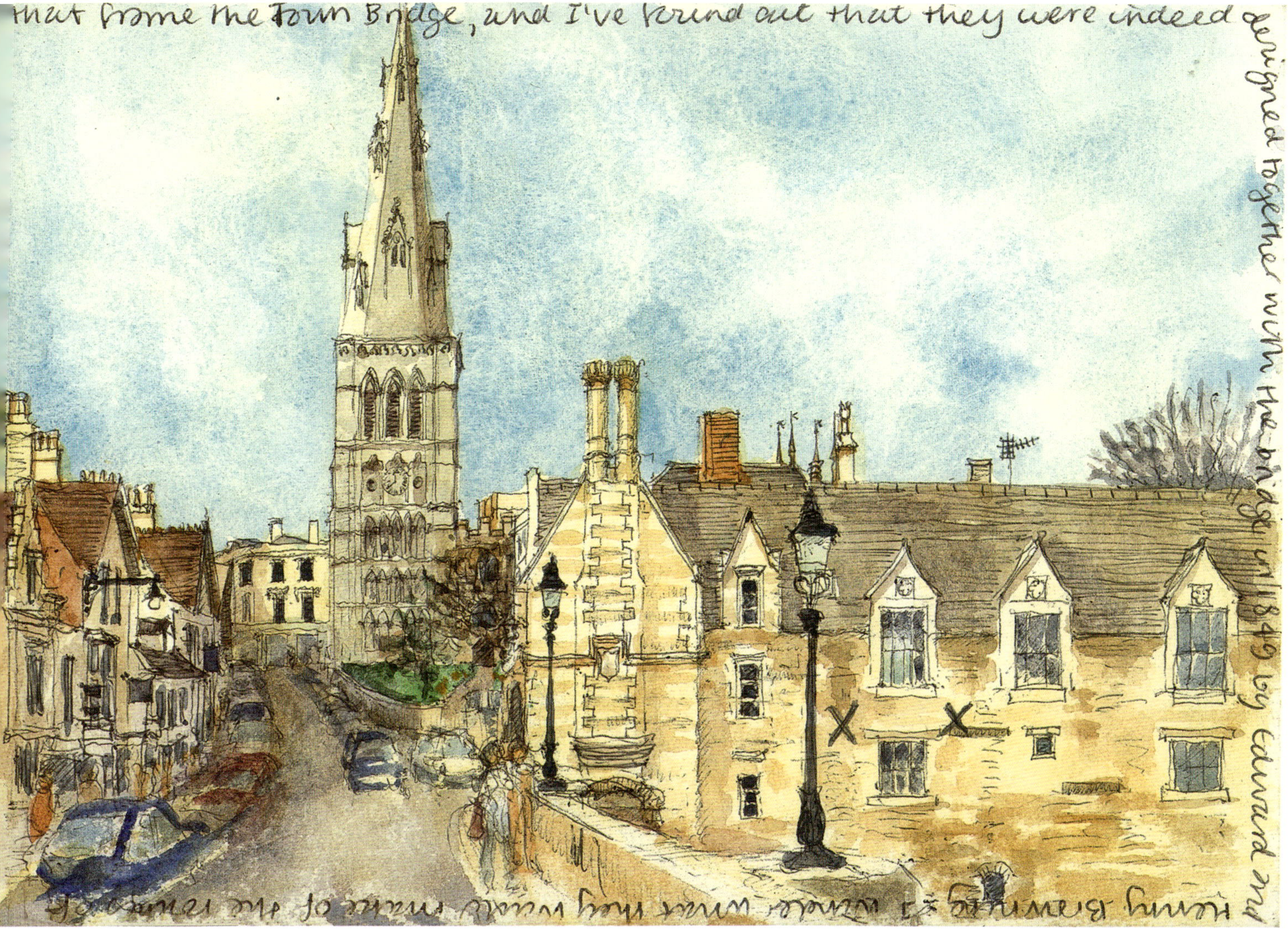
that frome the Town Bridge, and I've found out that they were indeed designed together with the bridge in 1849 by Edward and Henry Browning. I wonder what they made of the remains of

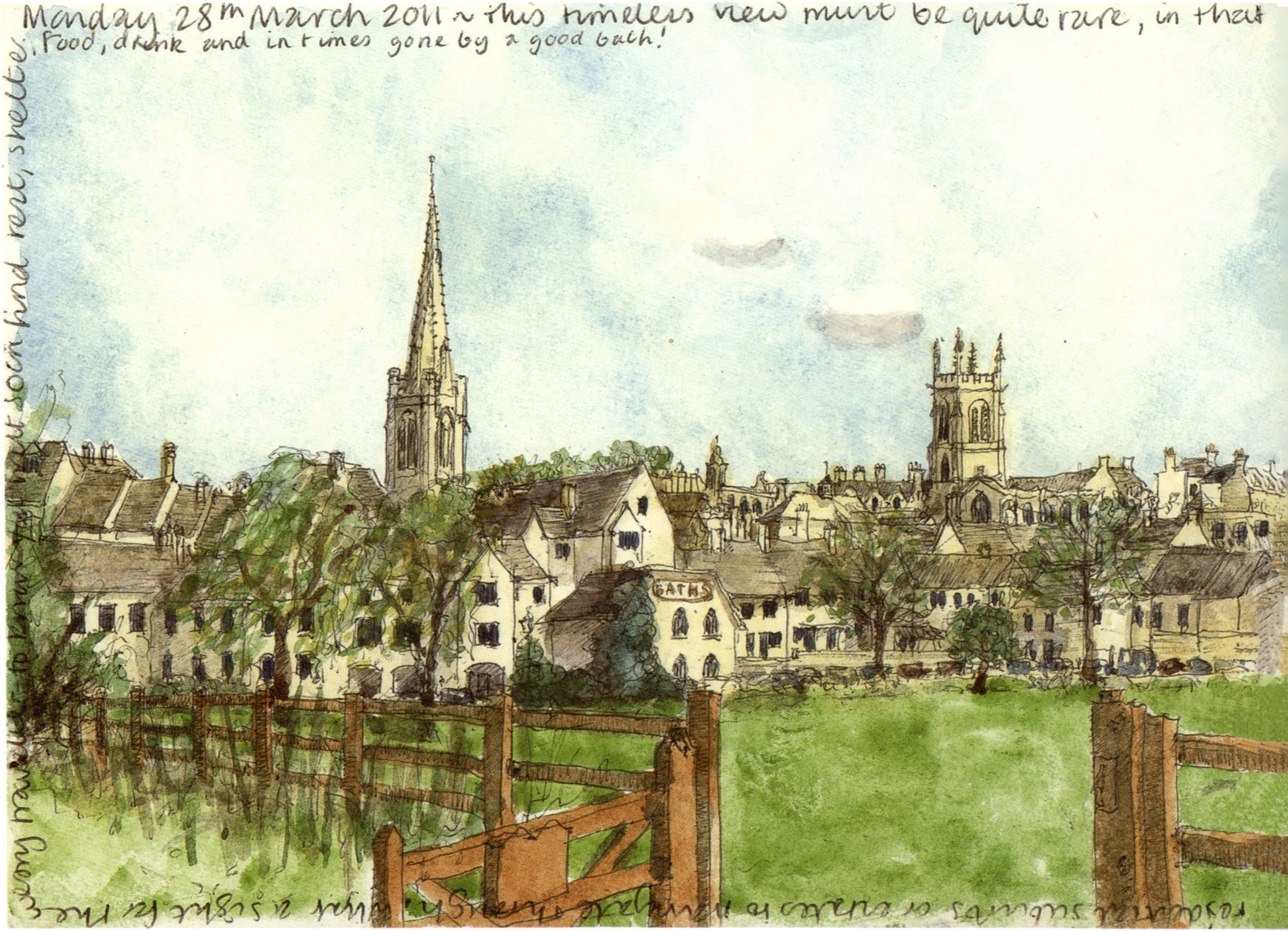
Monday 28th March 2011 ~ this timeless view must be quite rare, in that
residential suburbs or estates to navigate through. What a sight for the
weary traveller to know that will soon find rest, shelter,
Food, drink and in times gone by a good bath!

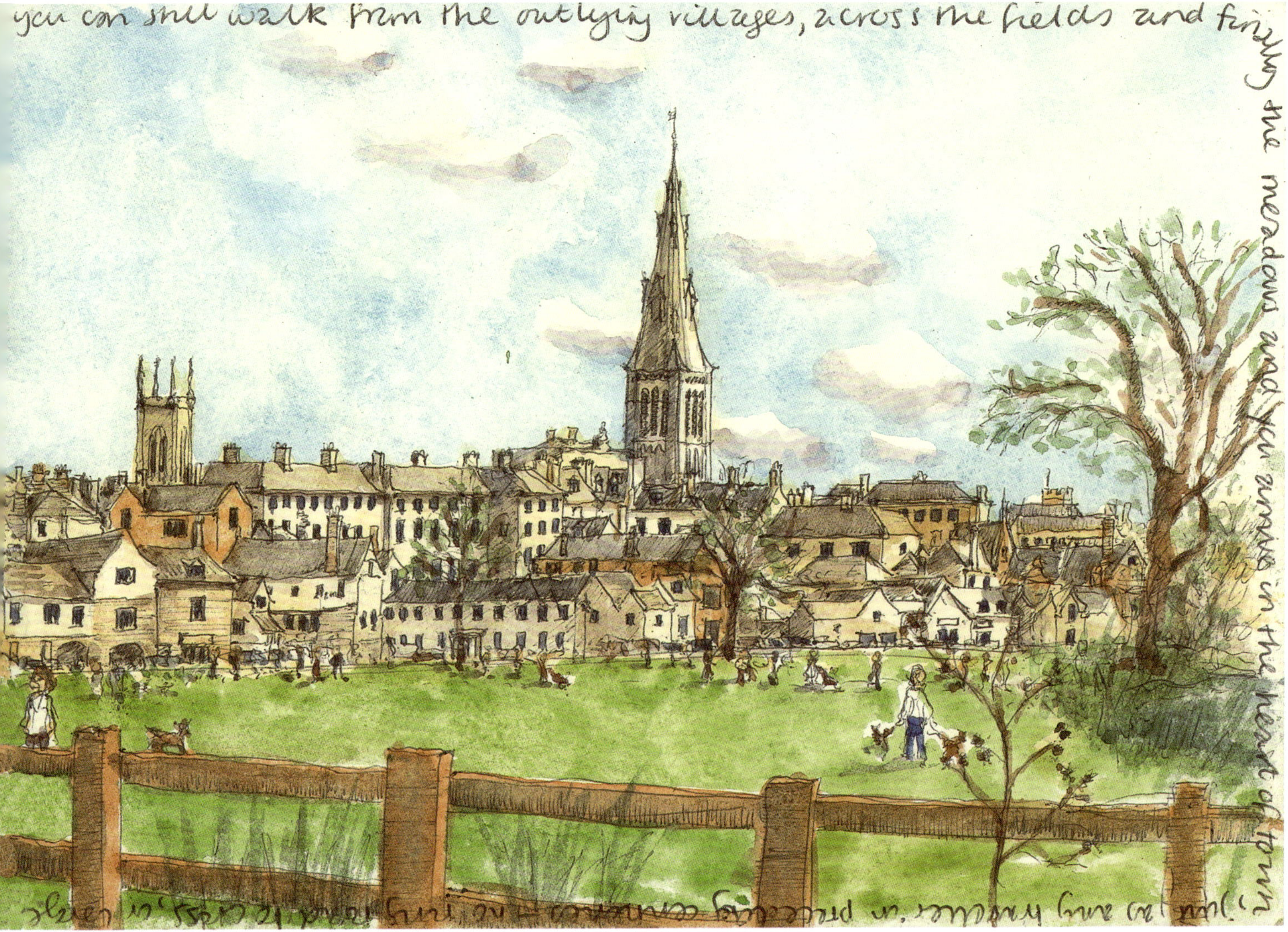
you can still walk from the outlying villages, across the fields and finally the meadows and you arrive in the heart of town, just as any traveller in preceding centuries – no busy road to cross, or large

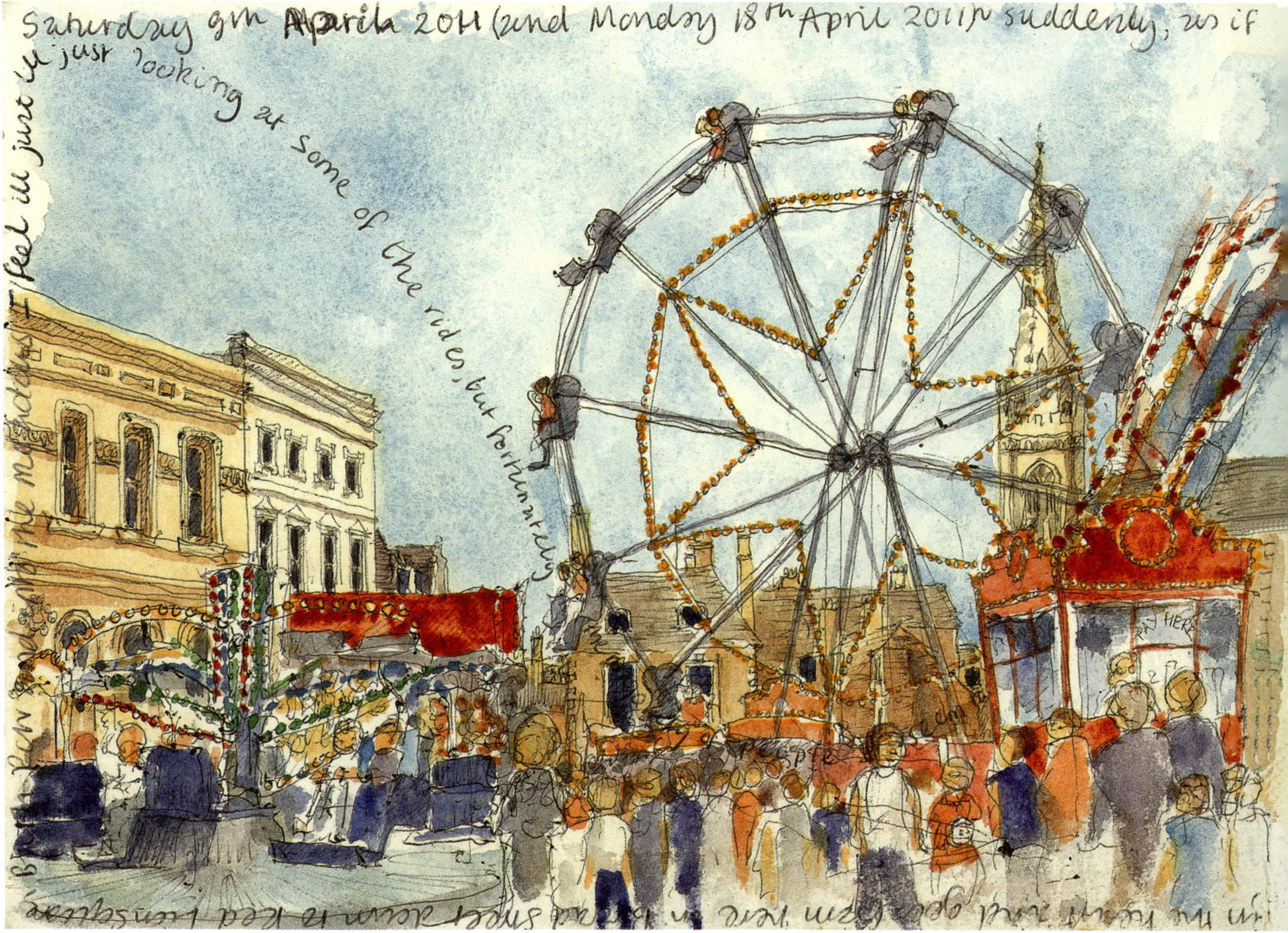
Saturday 9th April 2011 (and Monday 18th April 2011) suddenly, as if
Mondays I feel ill just
just looking at some of the rides, but fortunately
in the heart and go from here in Broad Street down to Red Lion Square

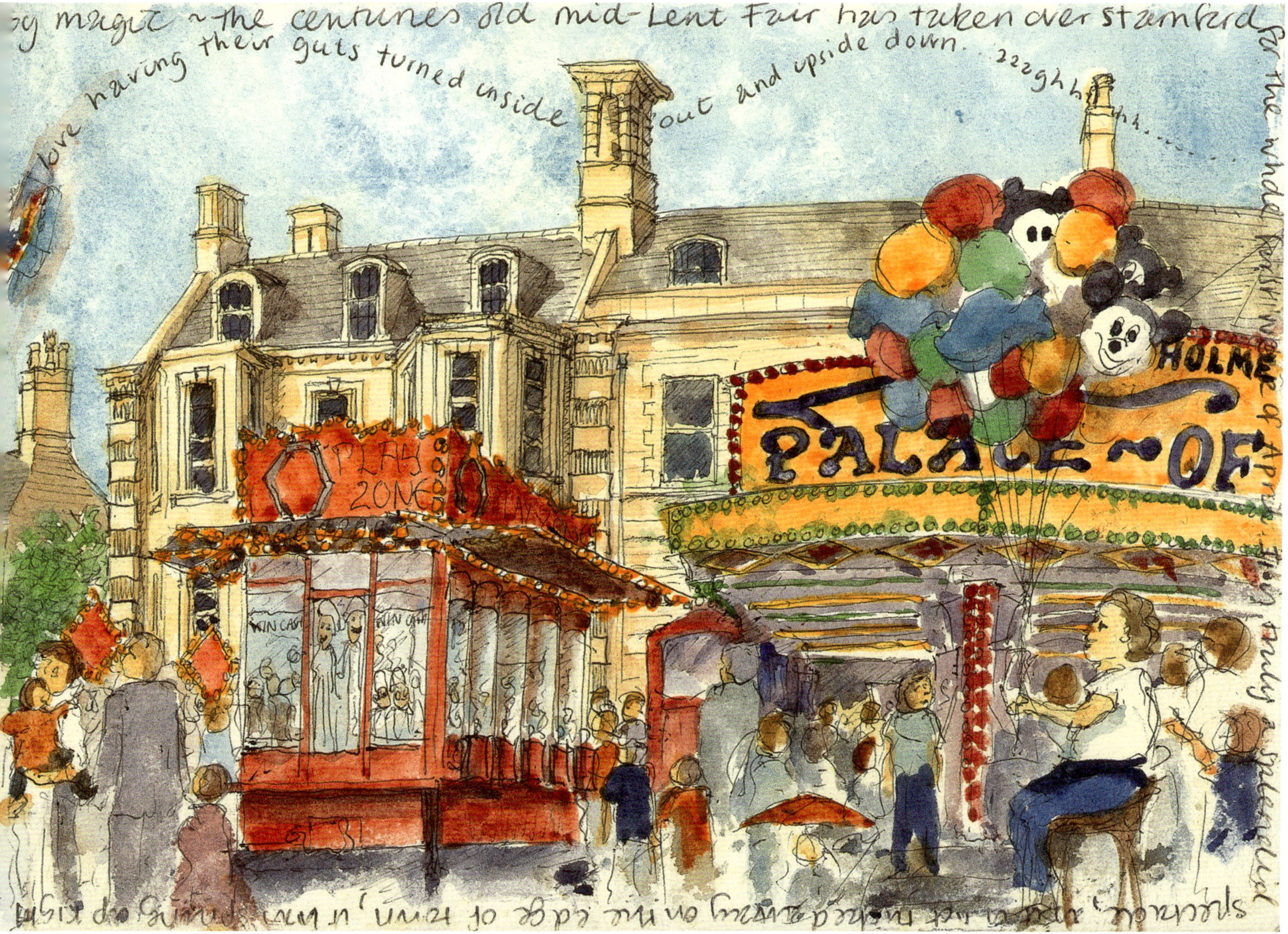
g magic ~ the centuries old mid-Lent Fair has taken over Stamford
love having their guts turned inside out and upside down.. aaarghhh......
PLAY ZONE
WIN CASH
HOLME
PALACE ~ OF

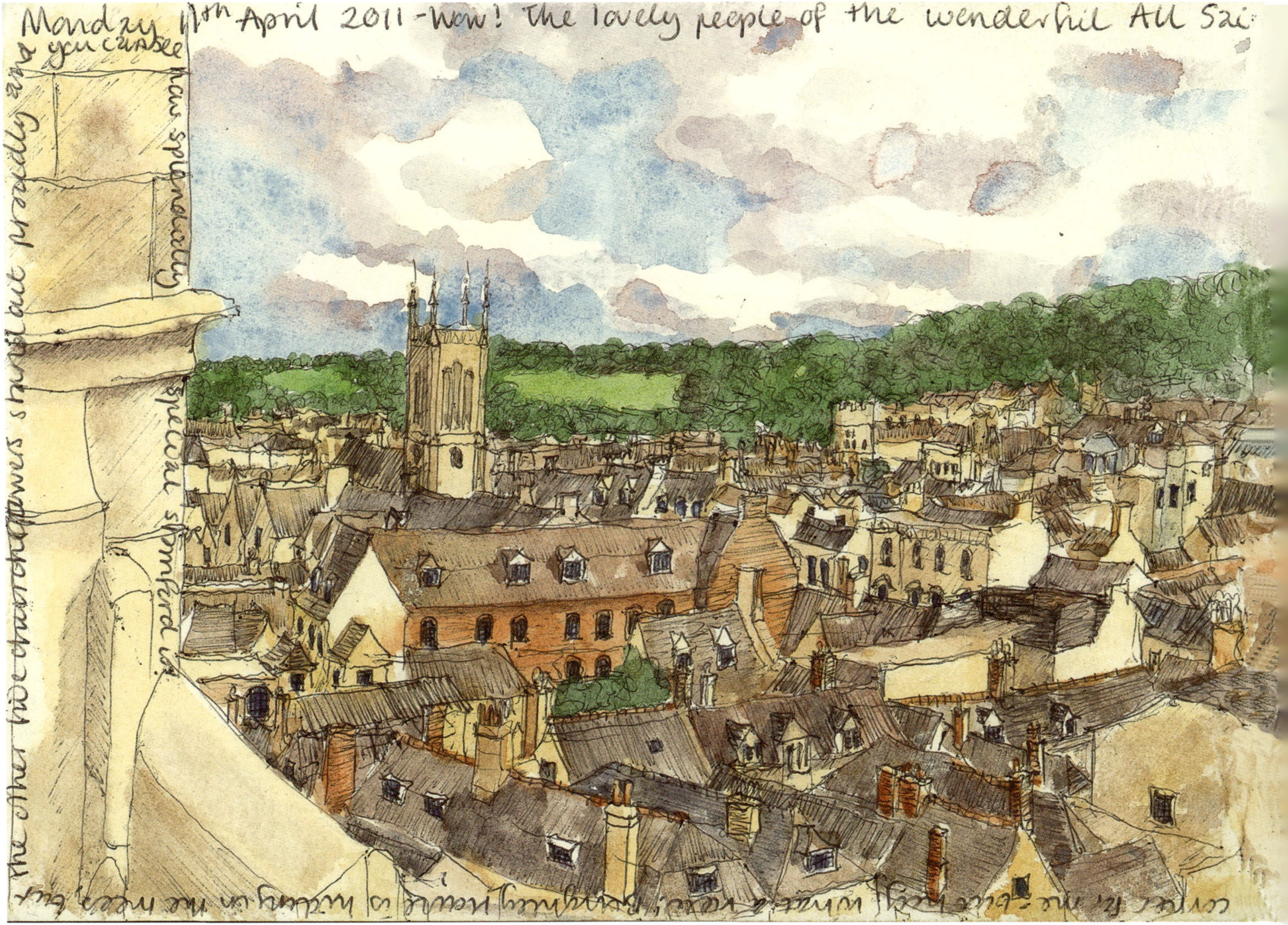
Monday 11th April 2011 - Wow! The lovely people of the wonderful All Sai
the other five church towers stand out proudly and you can see how splendidly special Stamford is

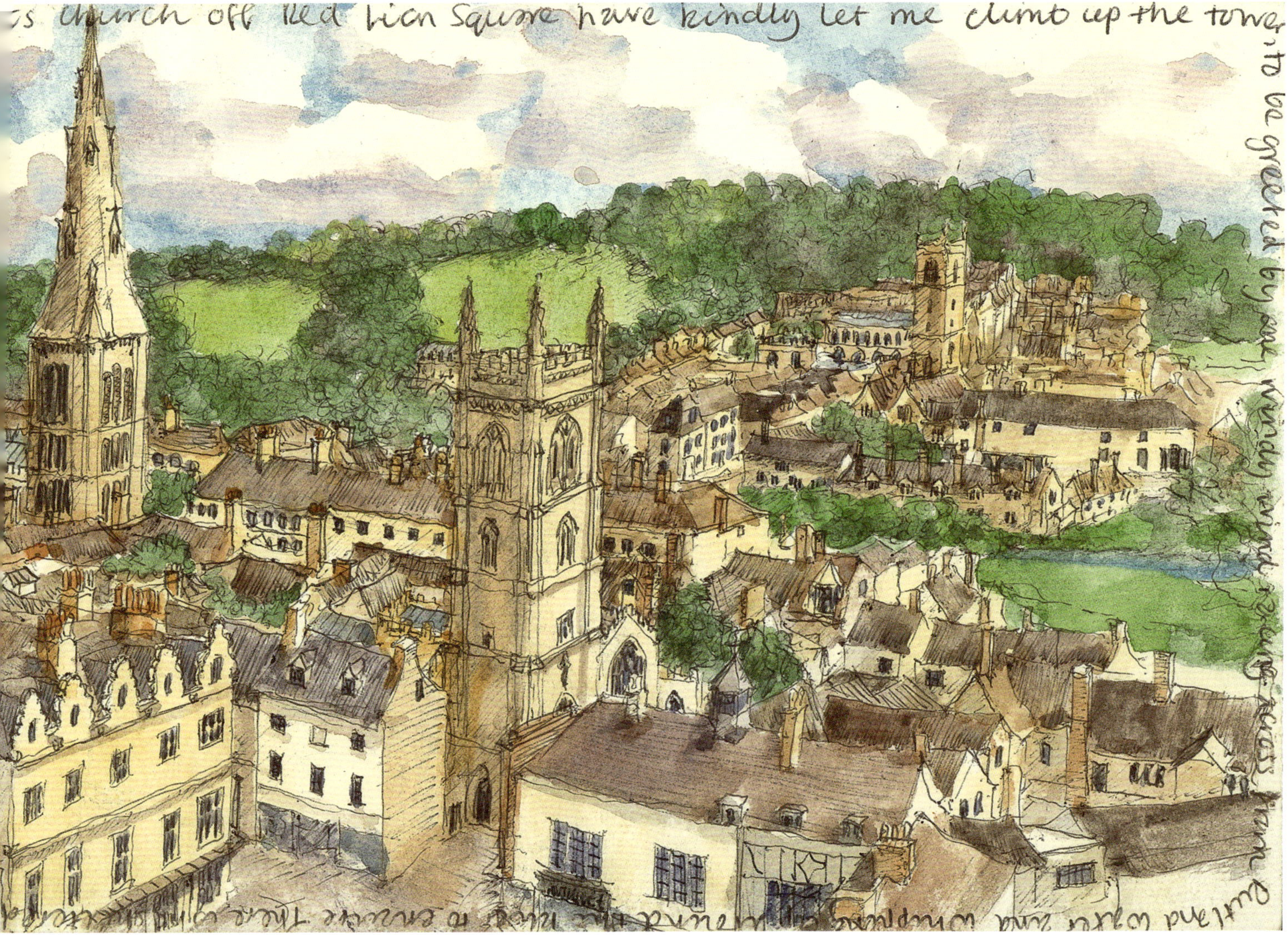
church off Red Lion Square have kindly let me climb up the tower
to be greeted by a windy wind racing across from

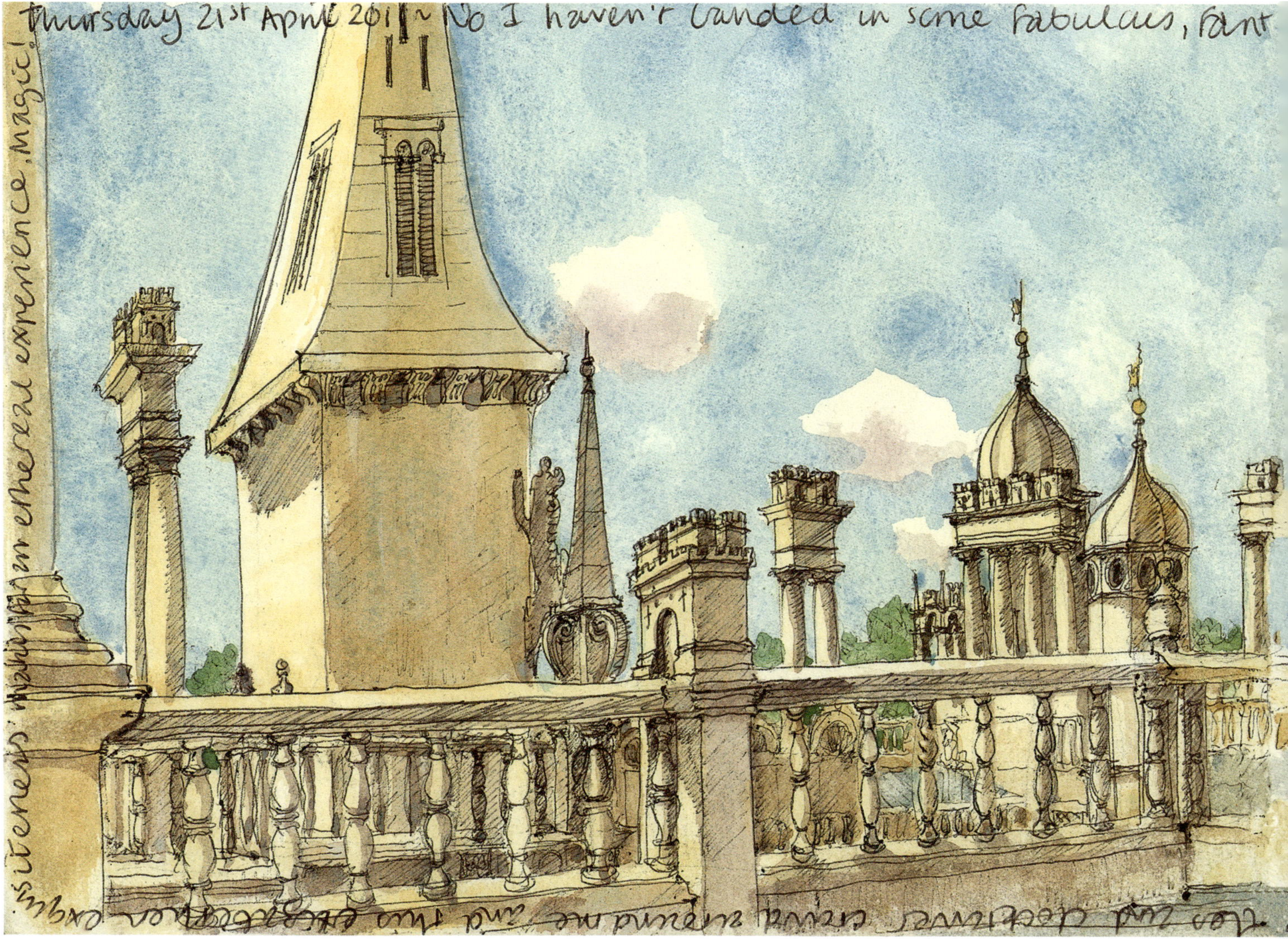
Thursday 21st April 2011 ~ No I haven't landed in some fabulous, fant
tles and clocktower crowd around me and this Elizabethan exquisiteness making an ethereal experience. Magic!

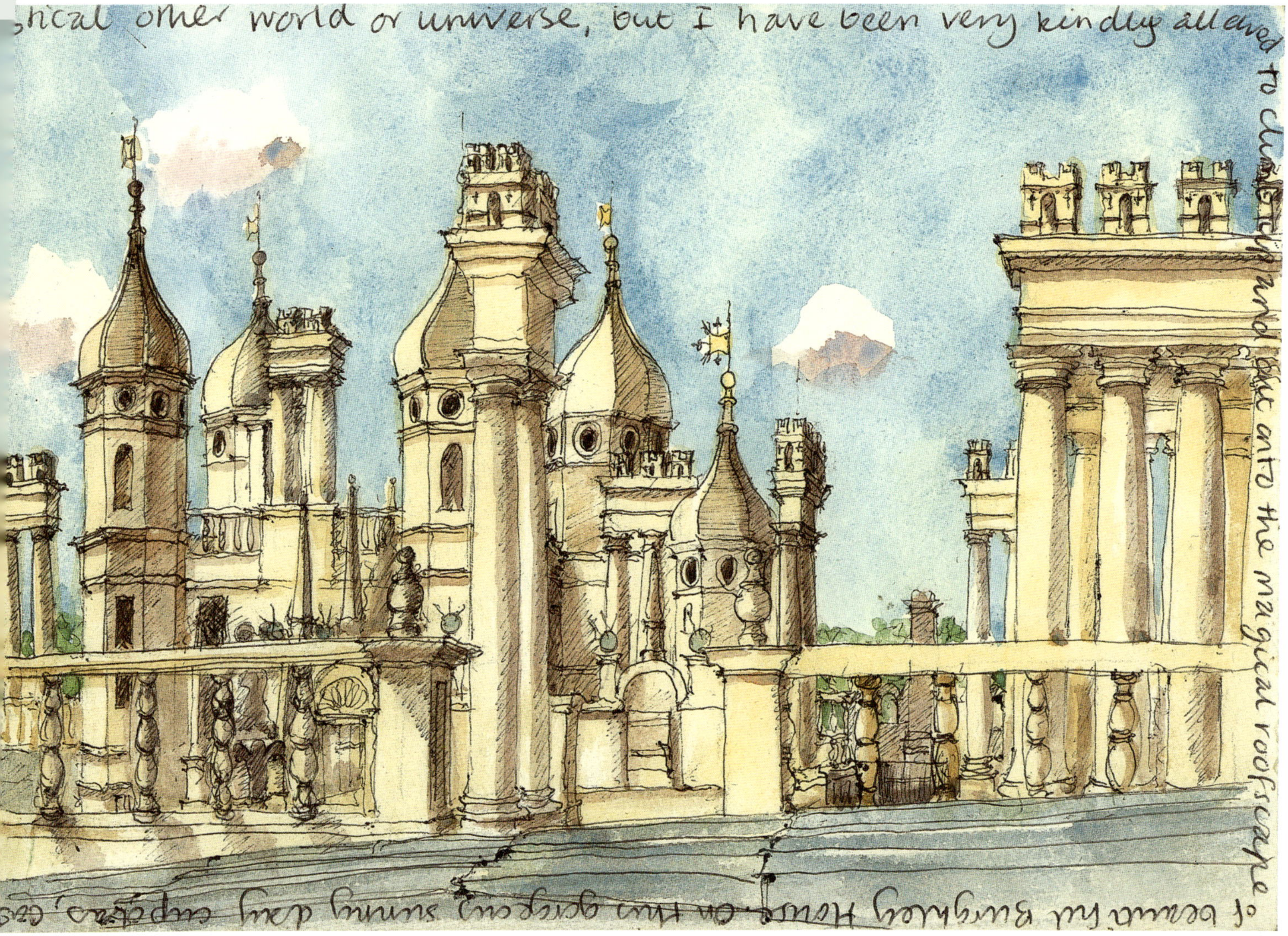
sical other world or universe, but I have been very kindly allowed
to climb up and out onto the magical roofscape
of beautiful Burghley House on this gorgeous sunny day cupolas, etc

Thursday 28th April and Thursday 2nd June 2011 - when in need of

through which you can see the deer and then suddenly there is

beautiful Burghley House, this effervescent Elizabethan

edifice and at either end of the wall you

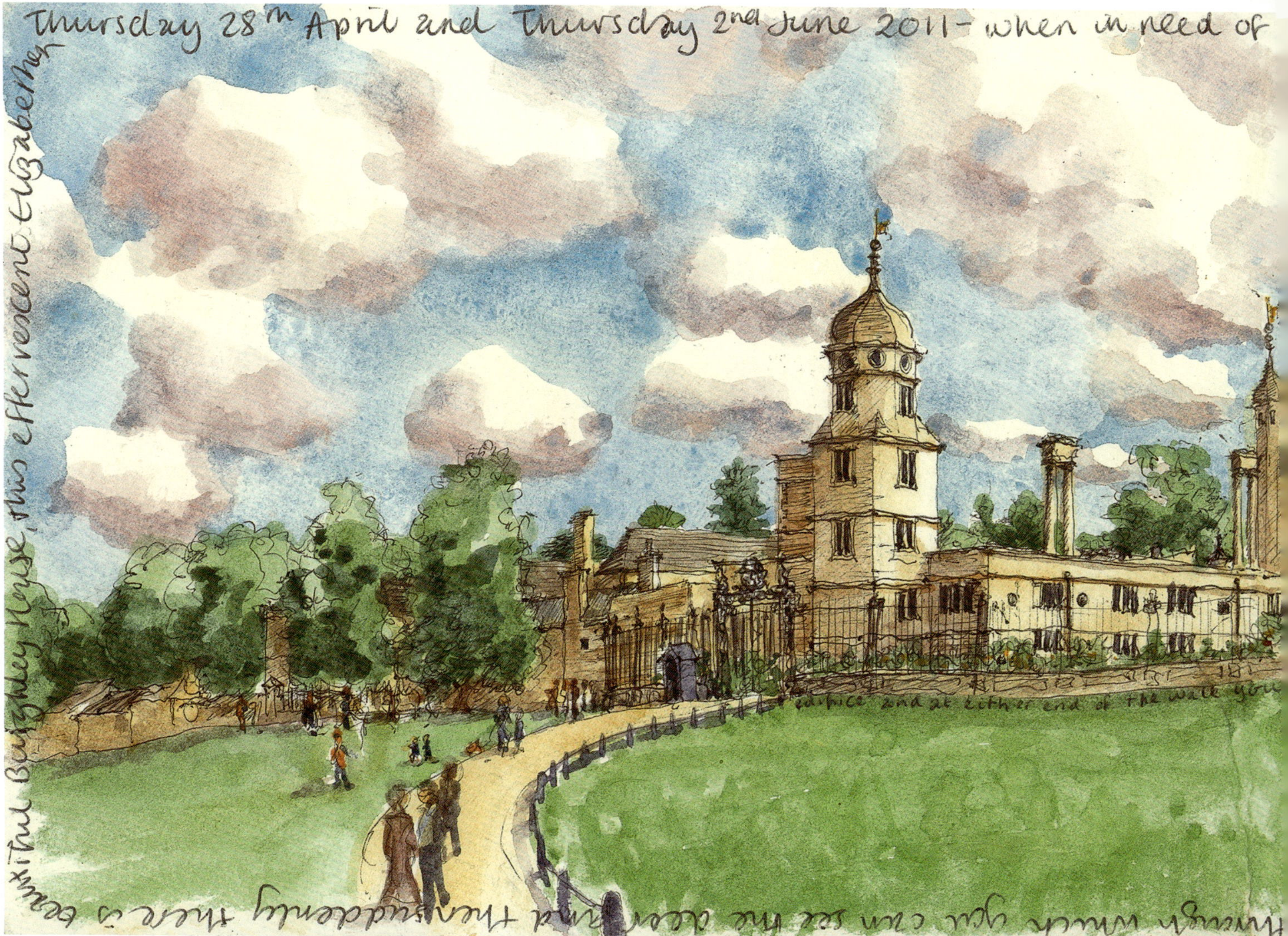

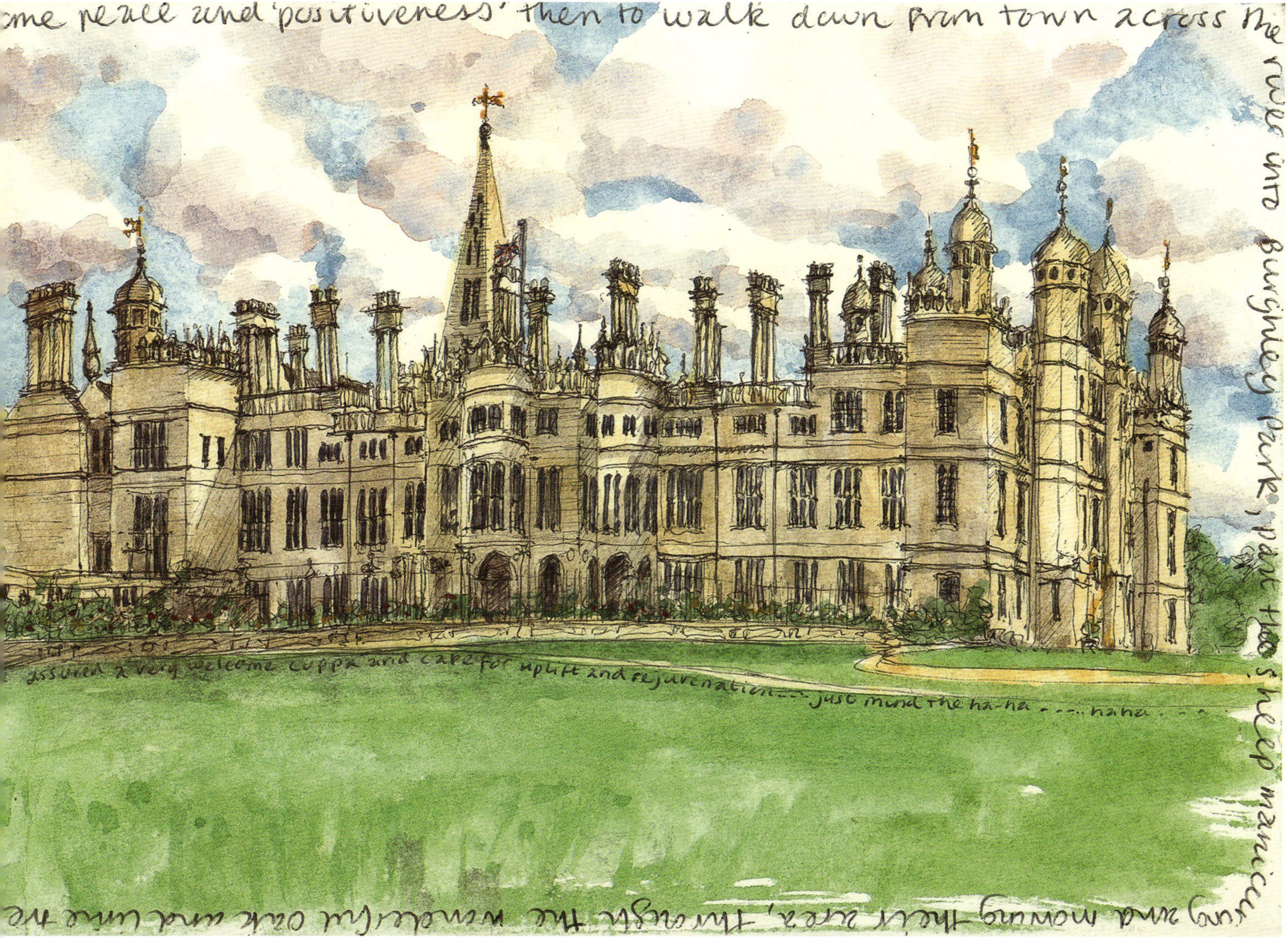
me peace and 'positiveness' then to walk down from town across the
river into Burghley Park, past the sheep munching and mowing their area, through the wonderful oak and lime tre
assured a very welcome cuppa and cake for uplift and rejuvenation... just mind the ha-ha .... haha ...

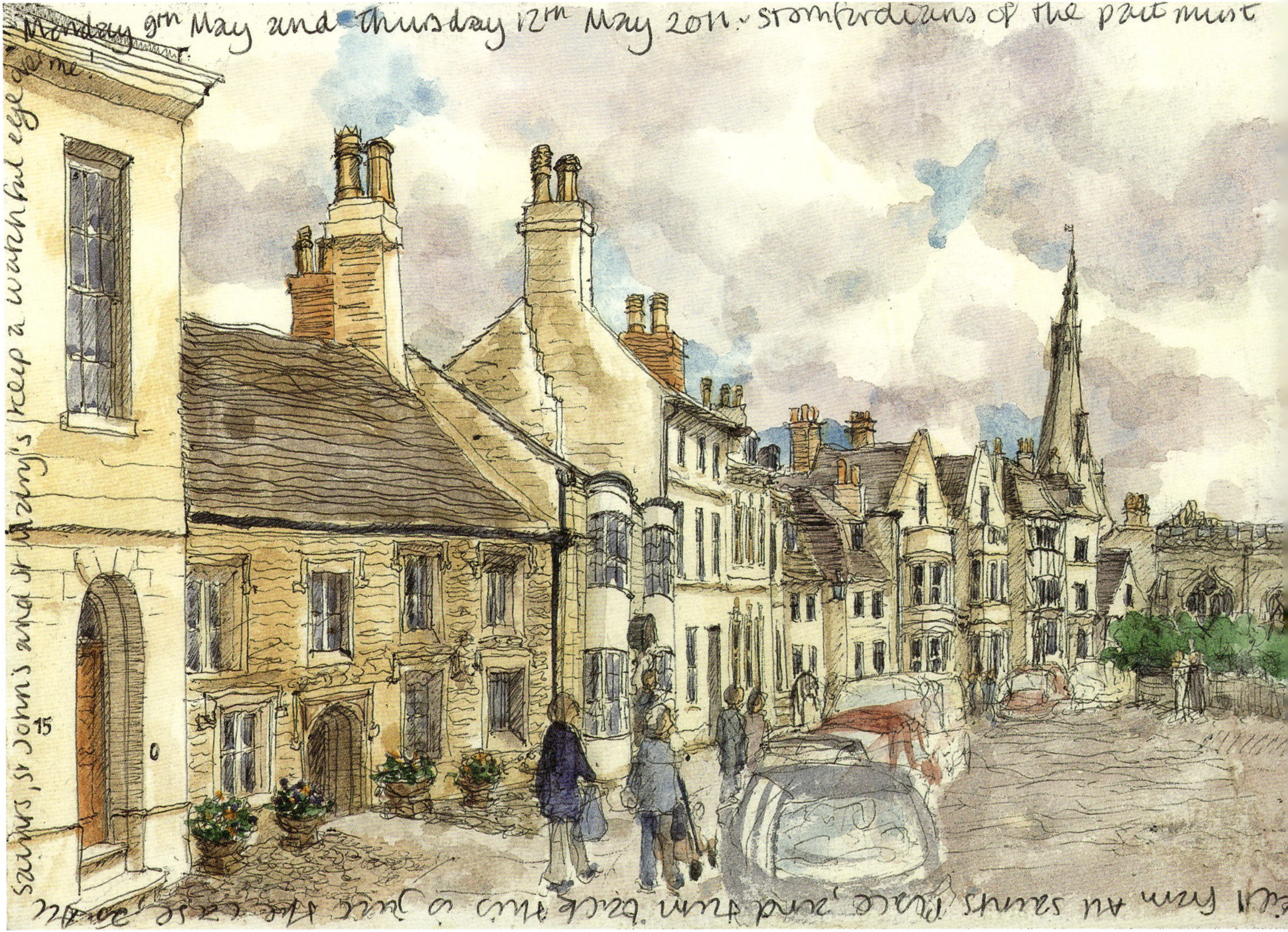
Monday 9th May and Thursday 12th May 2011. Stamfordians of the past must
saints, St John's and St Mary's keep a watchful eye on me!
15

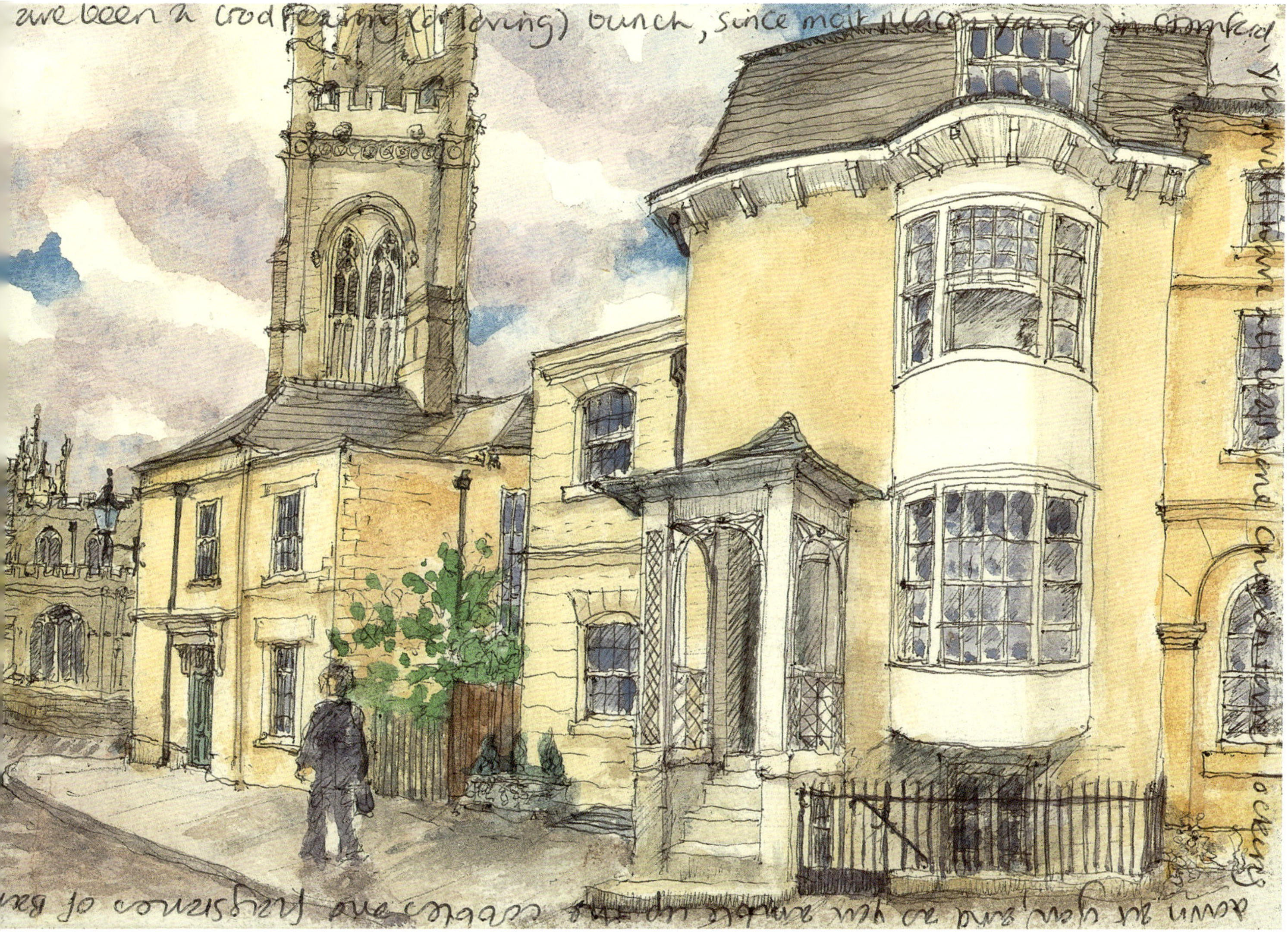
(or loving) bunch, since

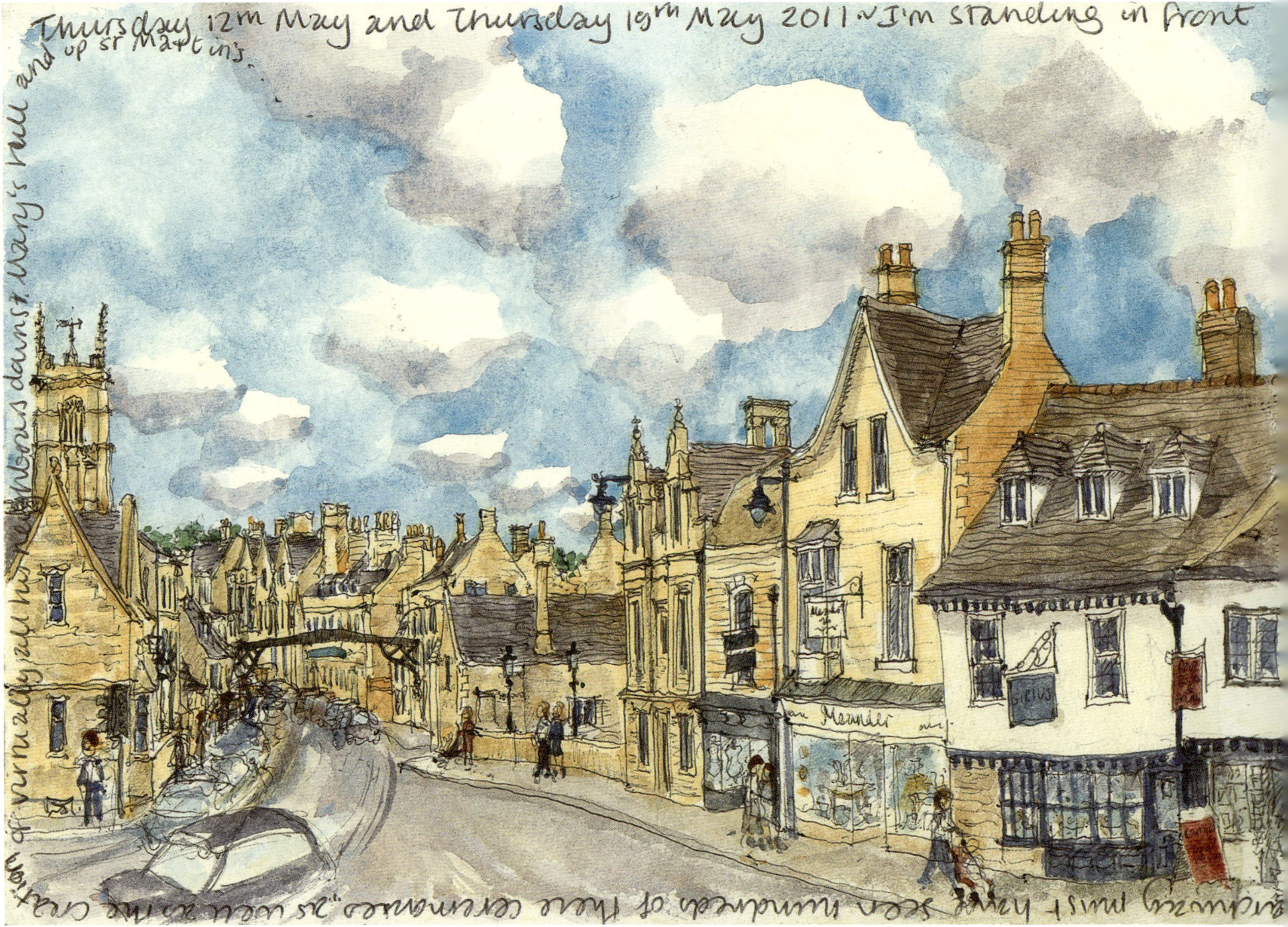
Thursday 12th May and Thursday 19th May 2011 ~ I'm standing in front
ancestry must have seen hundreds of these ceremonies" as well as the creation
of virtually all his neighbours down St Mary's hill and up St Martin's.

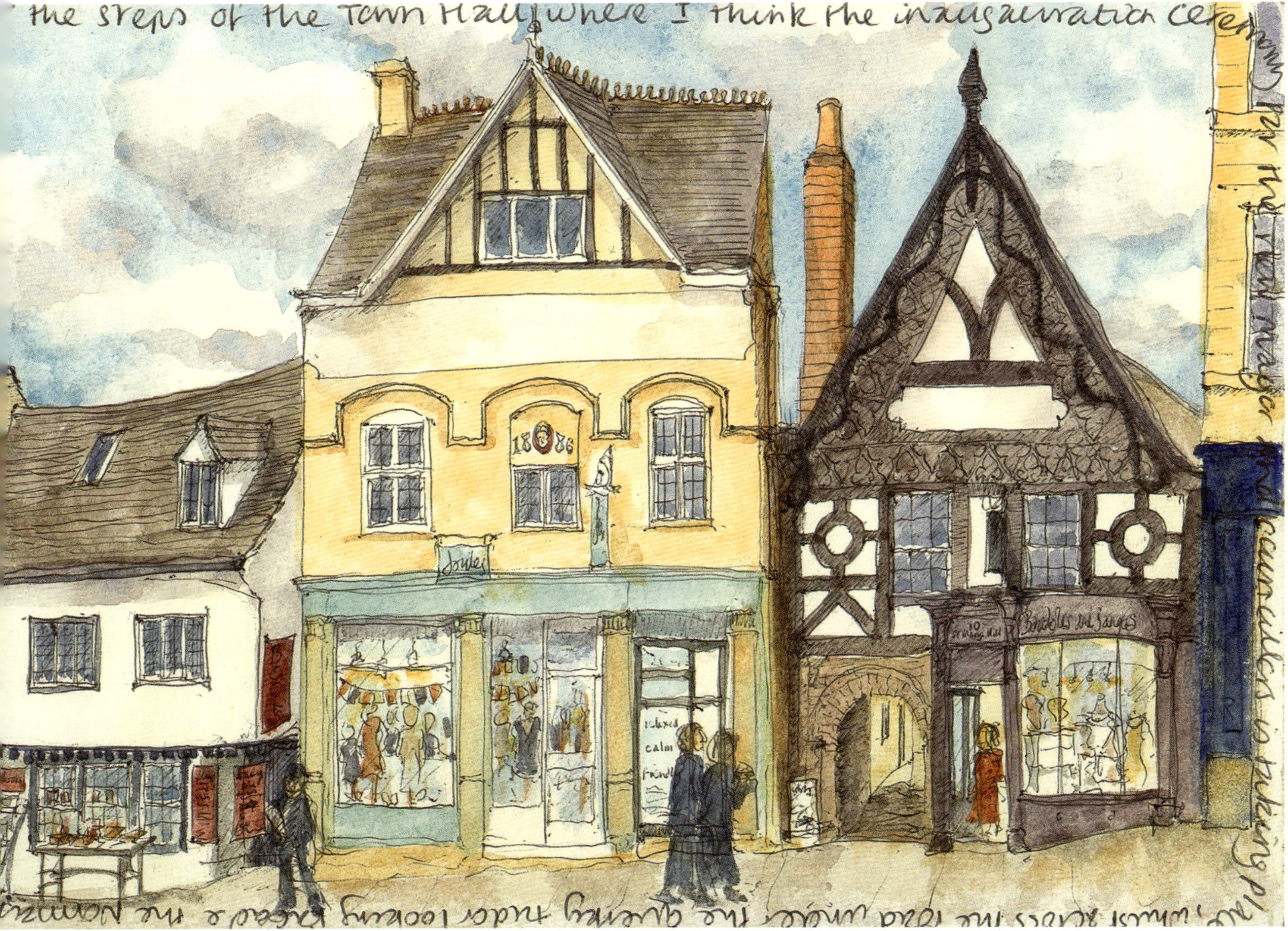
the steps of the Town Hall where I think the inaugauration cere
1886
Joules

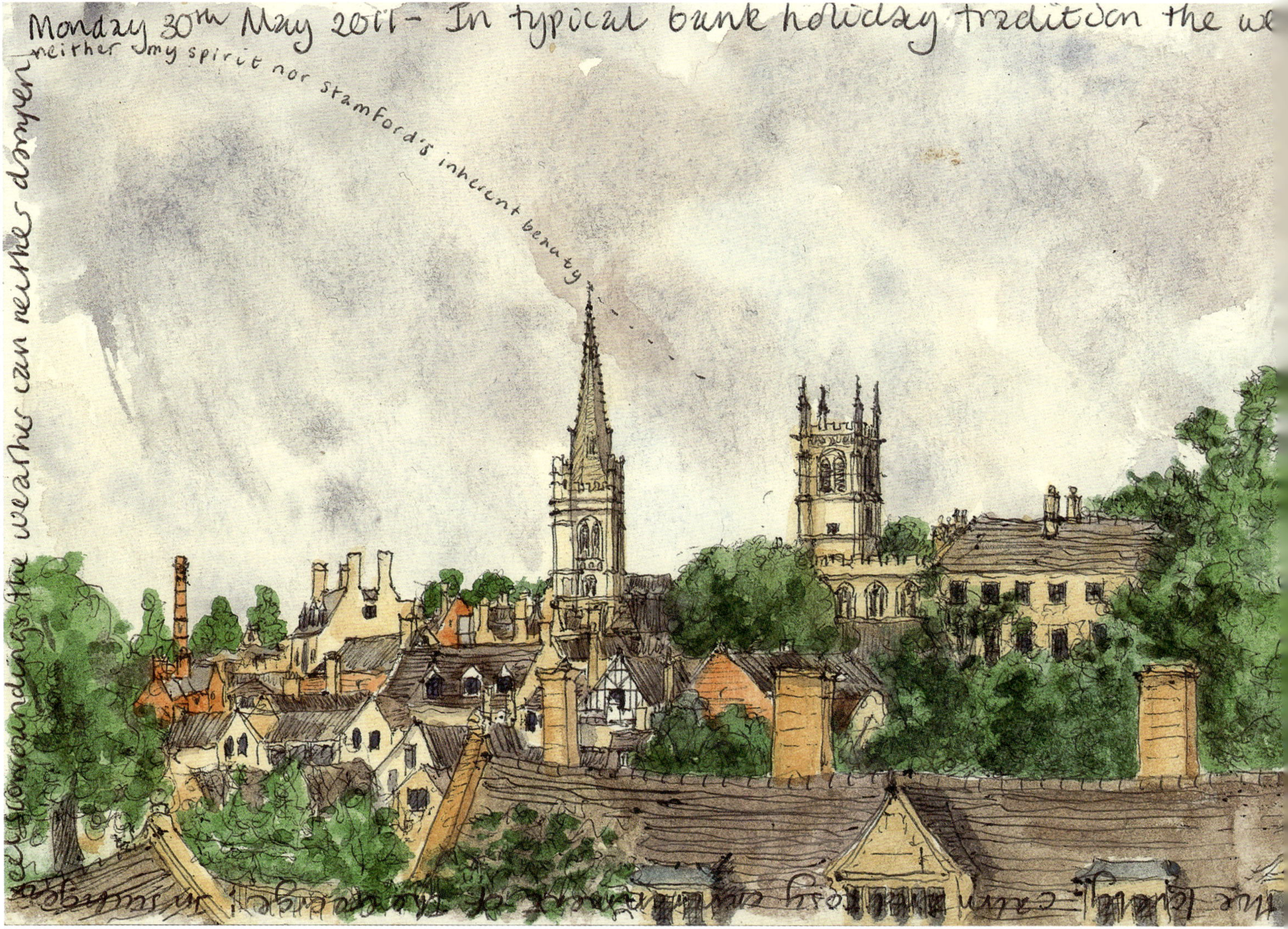
Monday 30th May 2011 - In typical bank holiday tradition the we
the weather can neither dampen
neither my spirit nor Stamford's inherent beauty

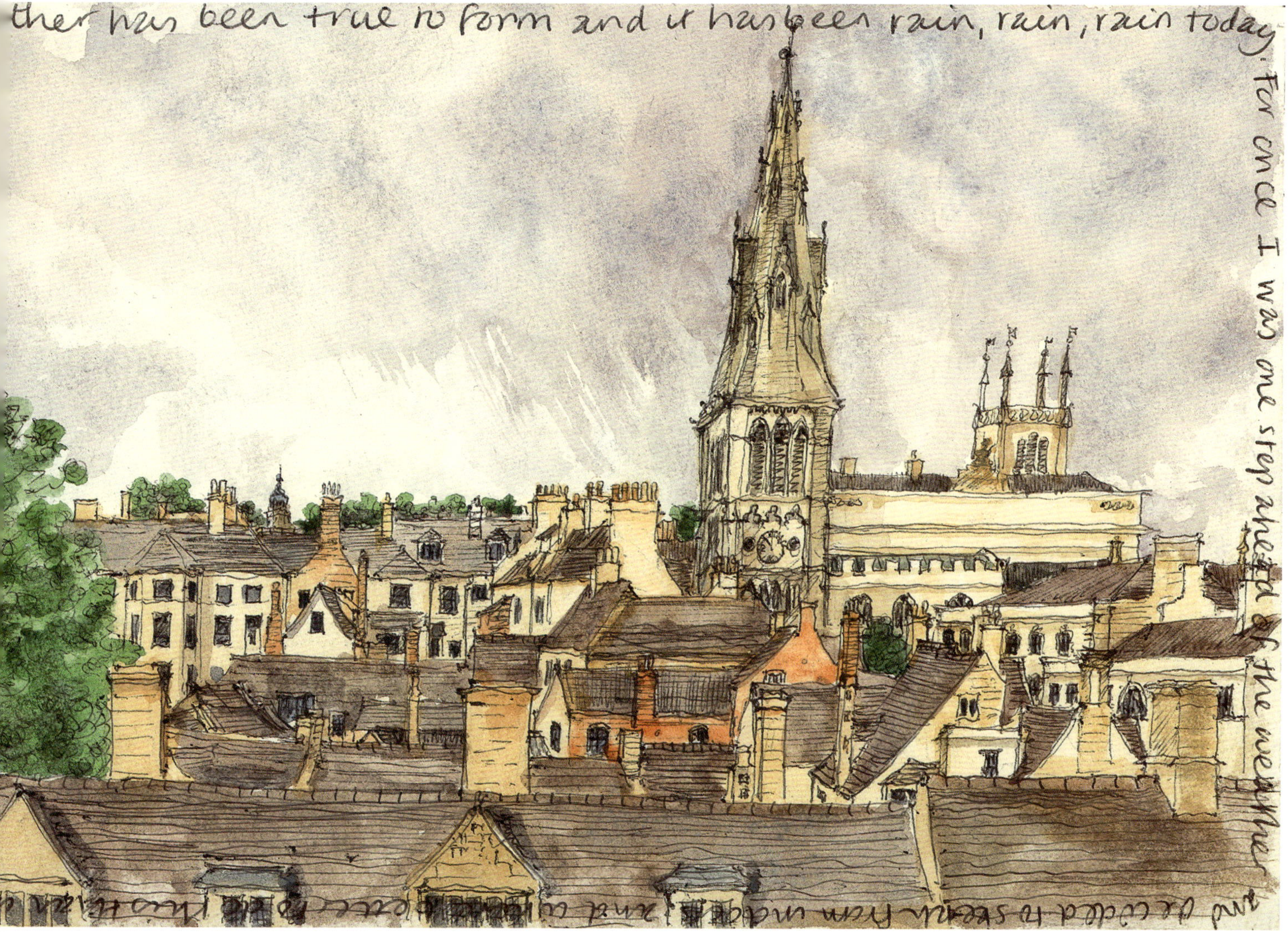
ther has been true to form and it has been rain, rain, rain today.
For once I was one step ahead of the weather
and decided to sketch from indoors, and

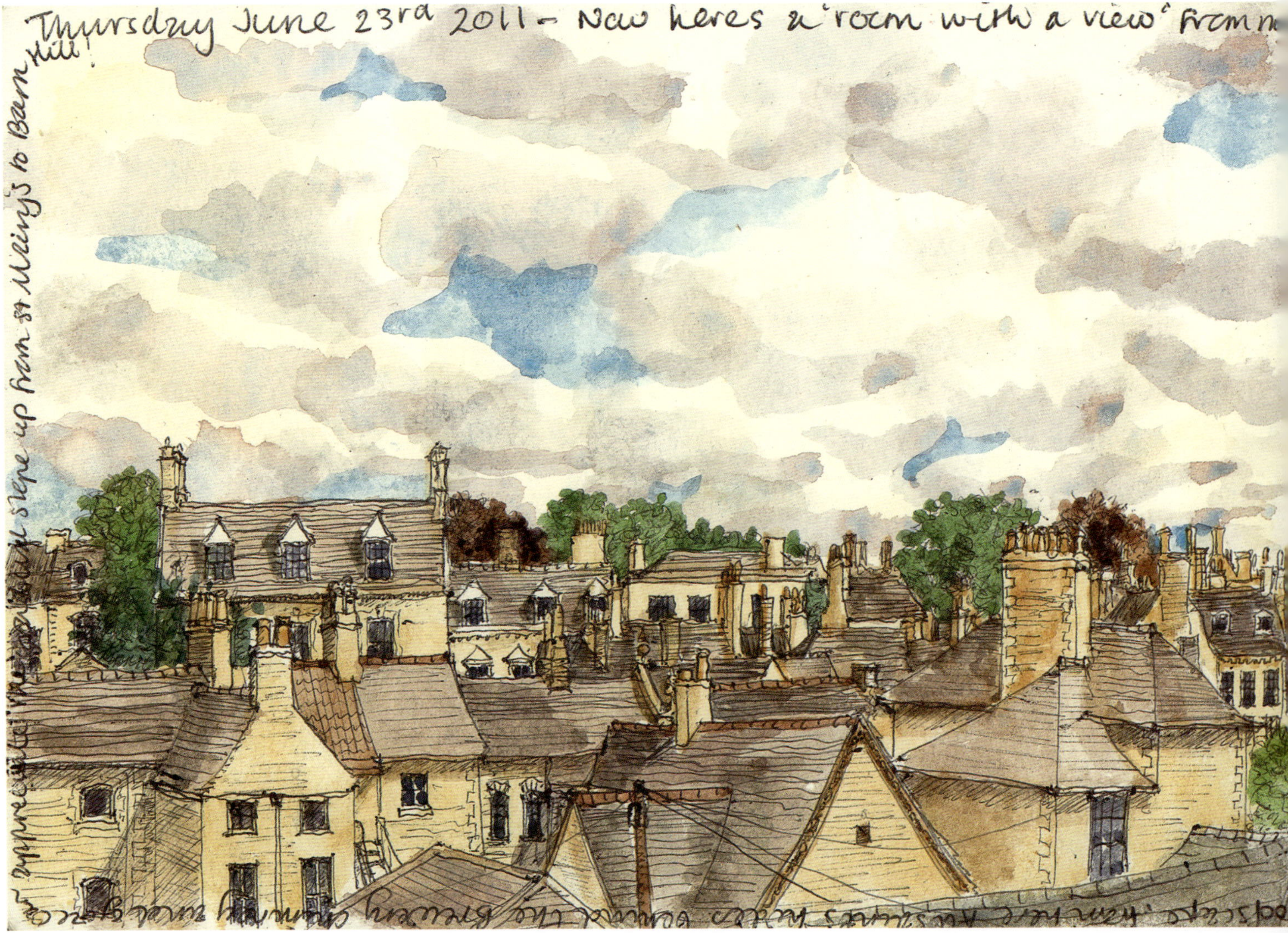
Thursday June 23rd 2011 – Now heres a 'room with a view' from m

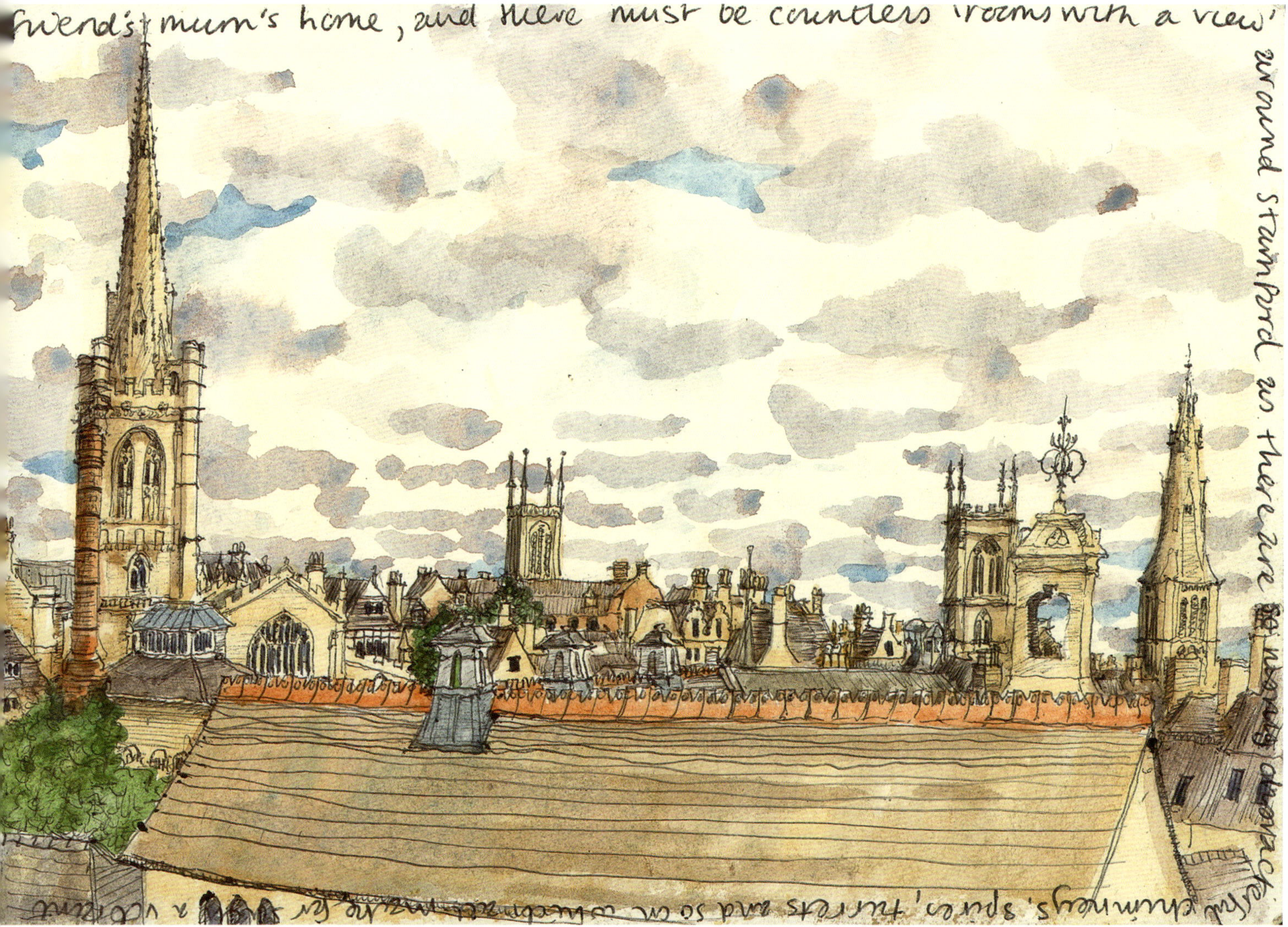
friend's mum's home, and there must be countless 'rooms with a view'
around Stamford as there are so many

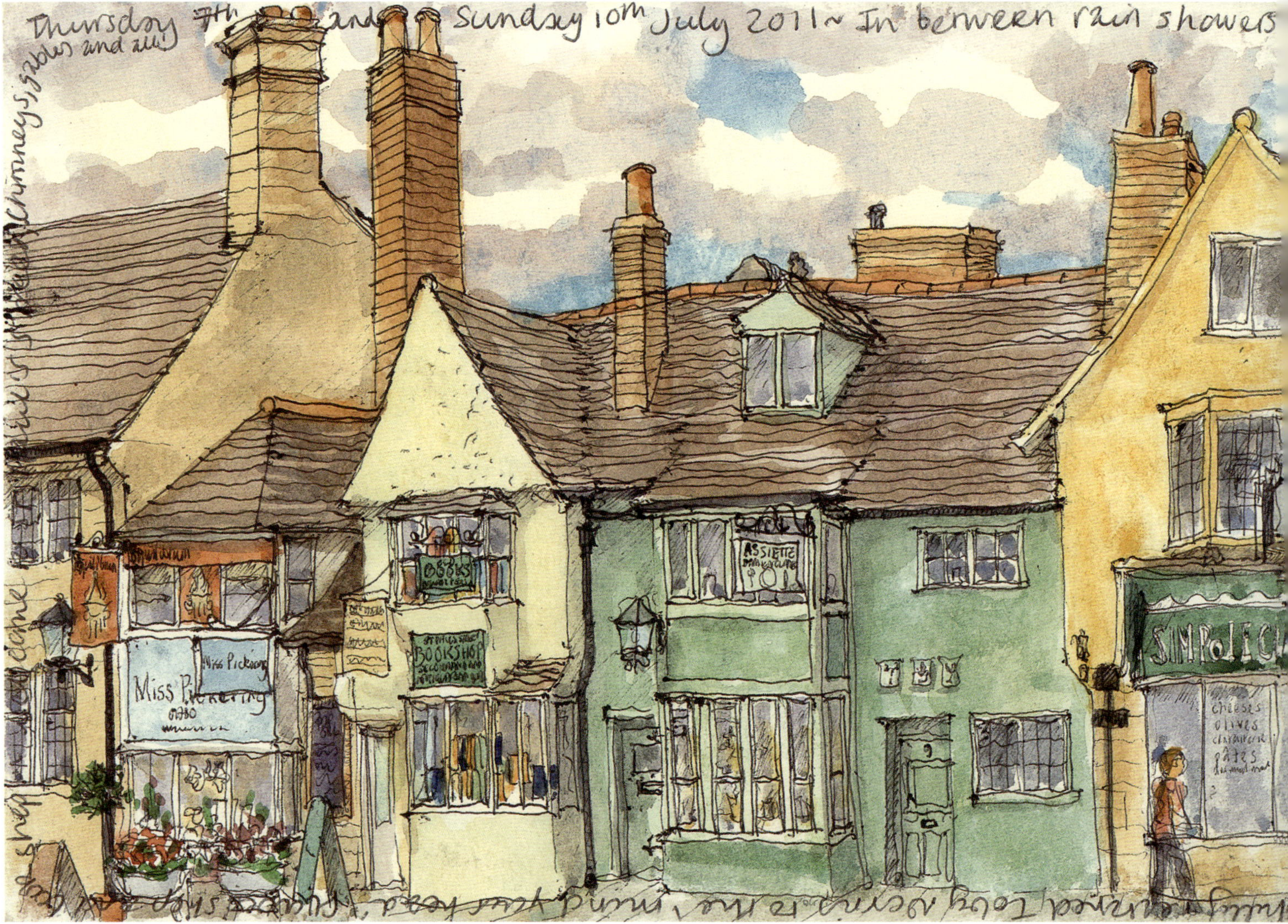
Thursday 7th and Sunday 10th July 2011 ~ In between rain showers
chimneys, gables and all
Miss Pickering
Miss Pickering
BOOKS
BOOKSHOP
ASSIETTE
SIMPOLE
cheeses
olives
pâtés

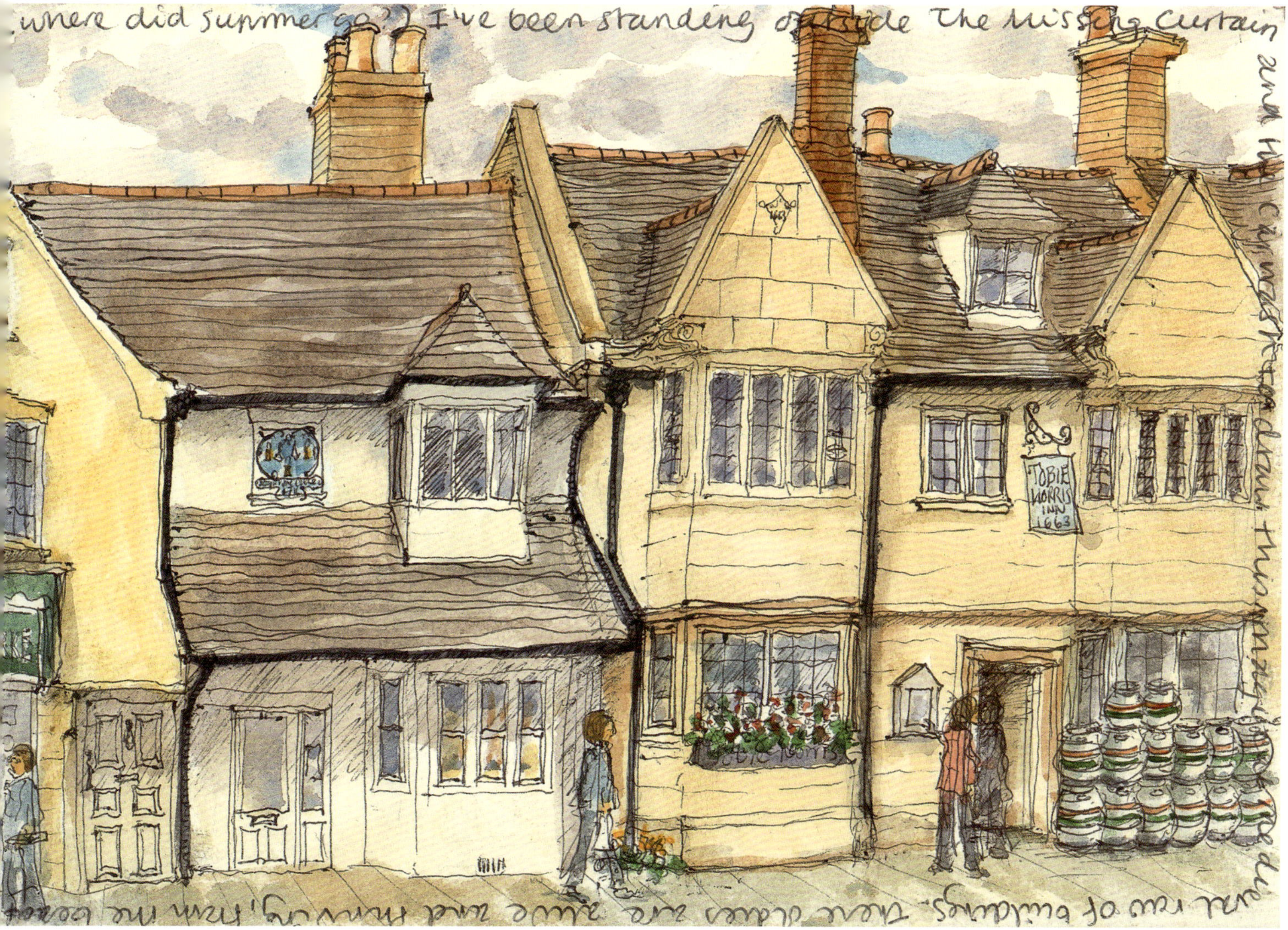
where did summer go?) I've been standing
TOBIE NORRIS INN 1663

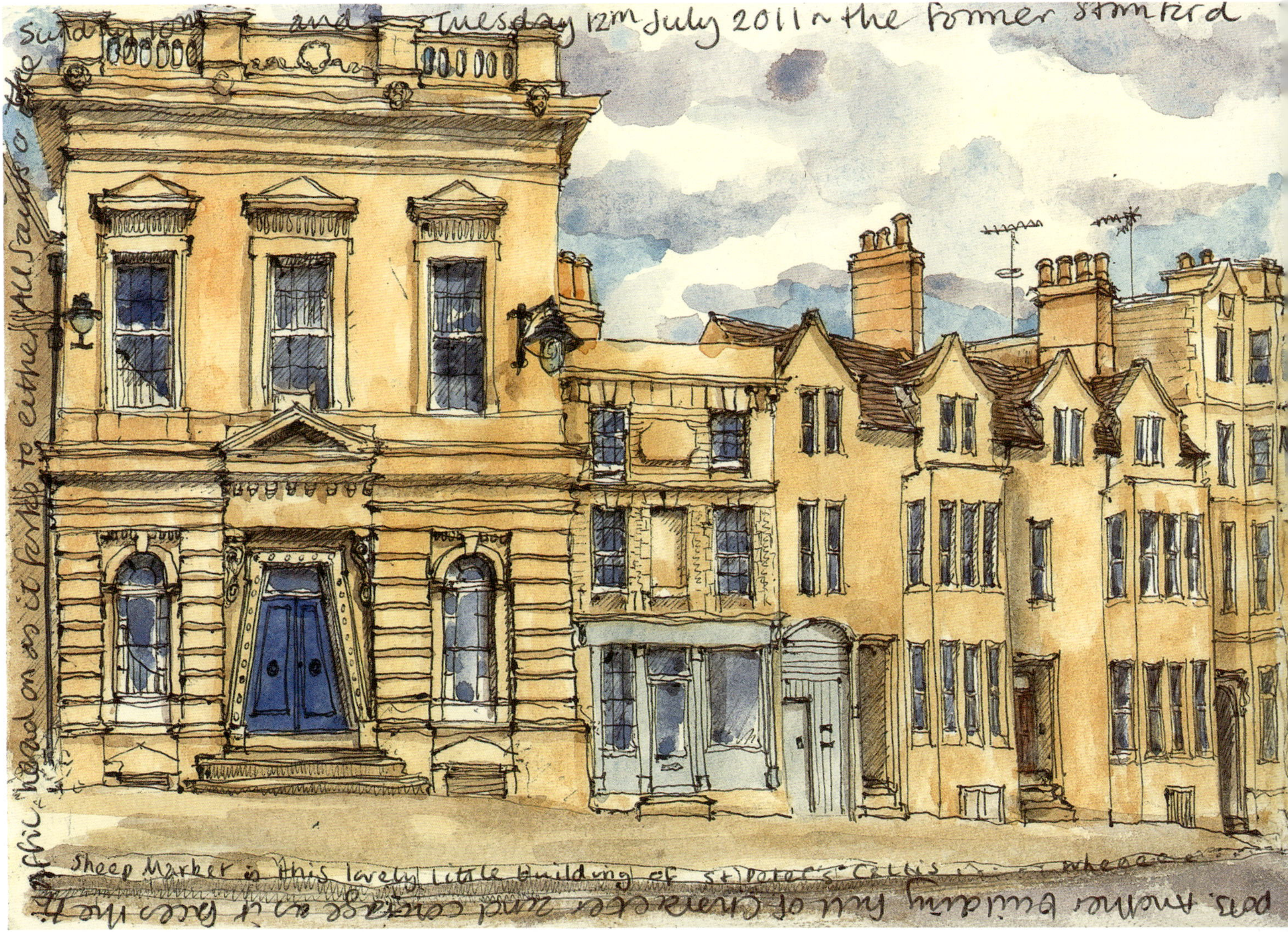
Tuesday 12th July 2011 ~ the former Stamford
Sheep Market is this lovely little building of St Peter's Callis
as it forks to either All Saints or the

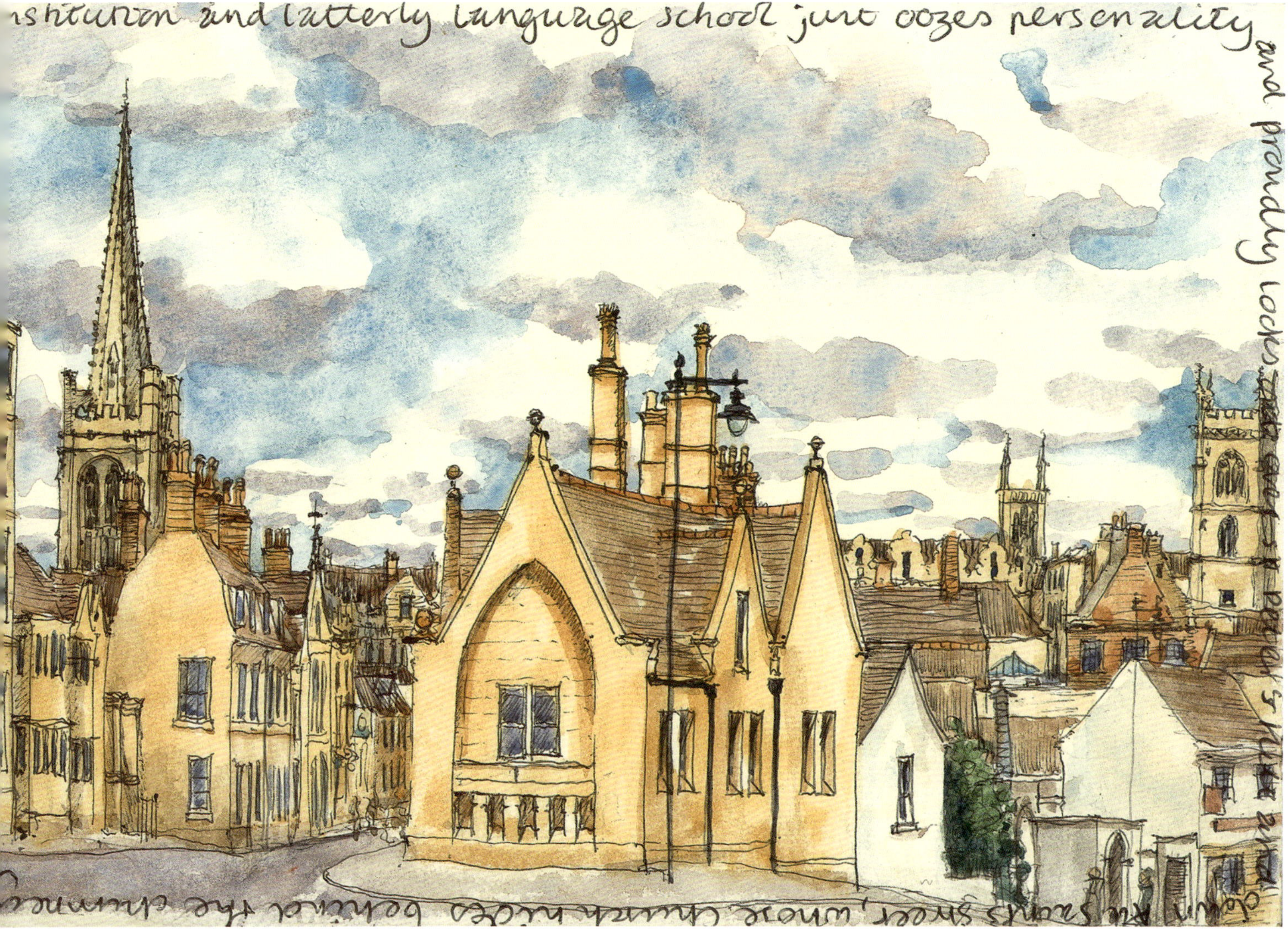
and latterly language school just oozes personality

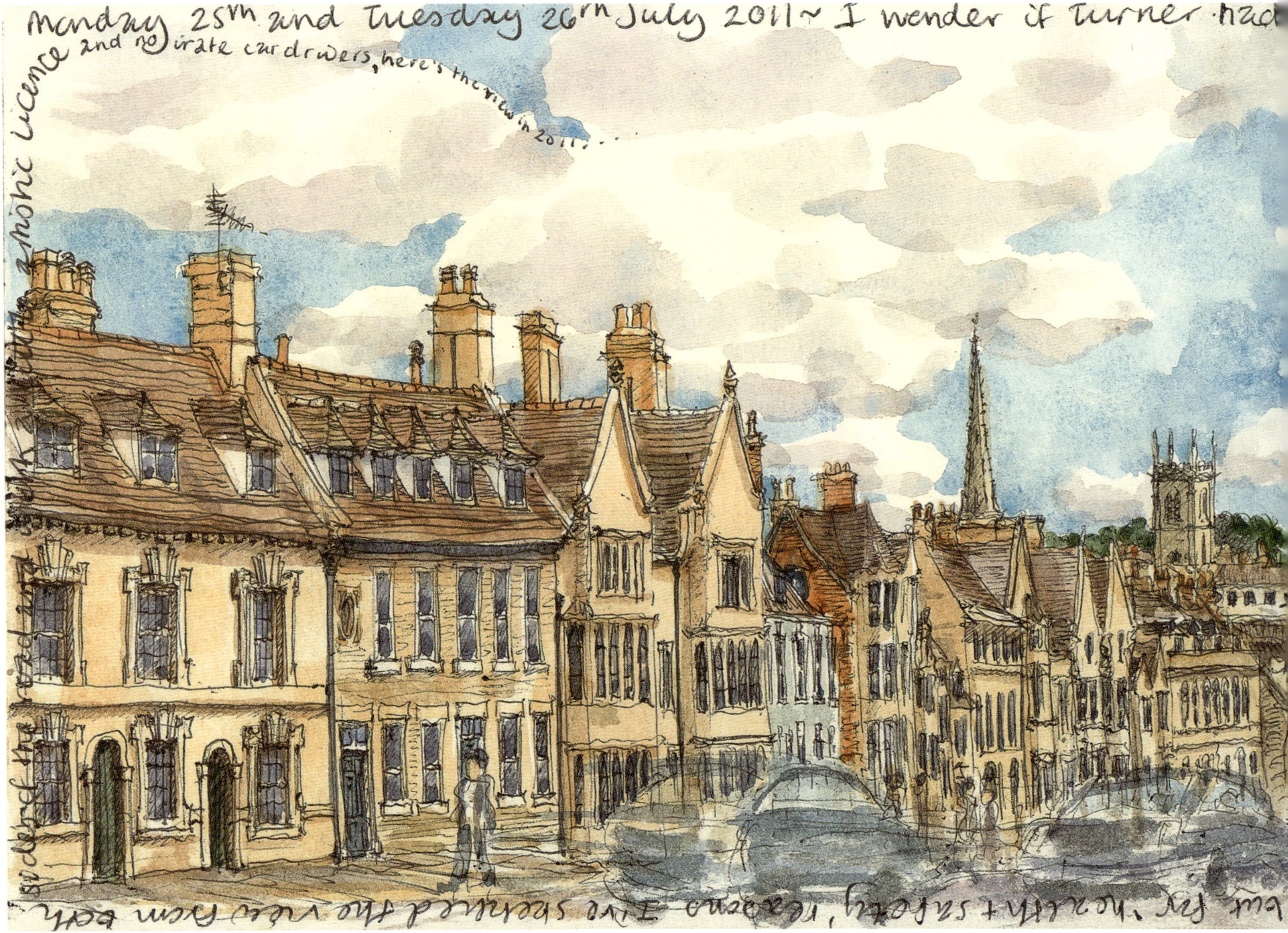
Monday 25th and Tuesday 26th July 2011 ~ I wonder if Turner had
licence and no irate car drivers, here's the view in 2011 . . .
but for 'health + safety' reasons I've sketched the view from both

o dodge lots of horses, carts and carriages when he created his wonderful view looking down High Street St Martins. Ideally I would have stood in the middle of the pelican crossi

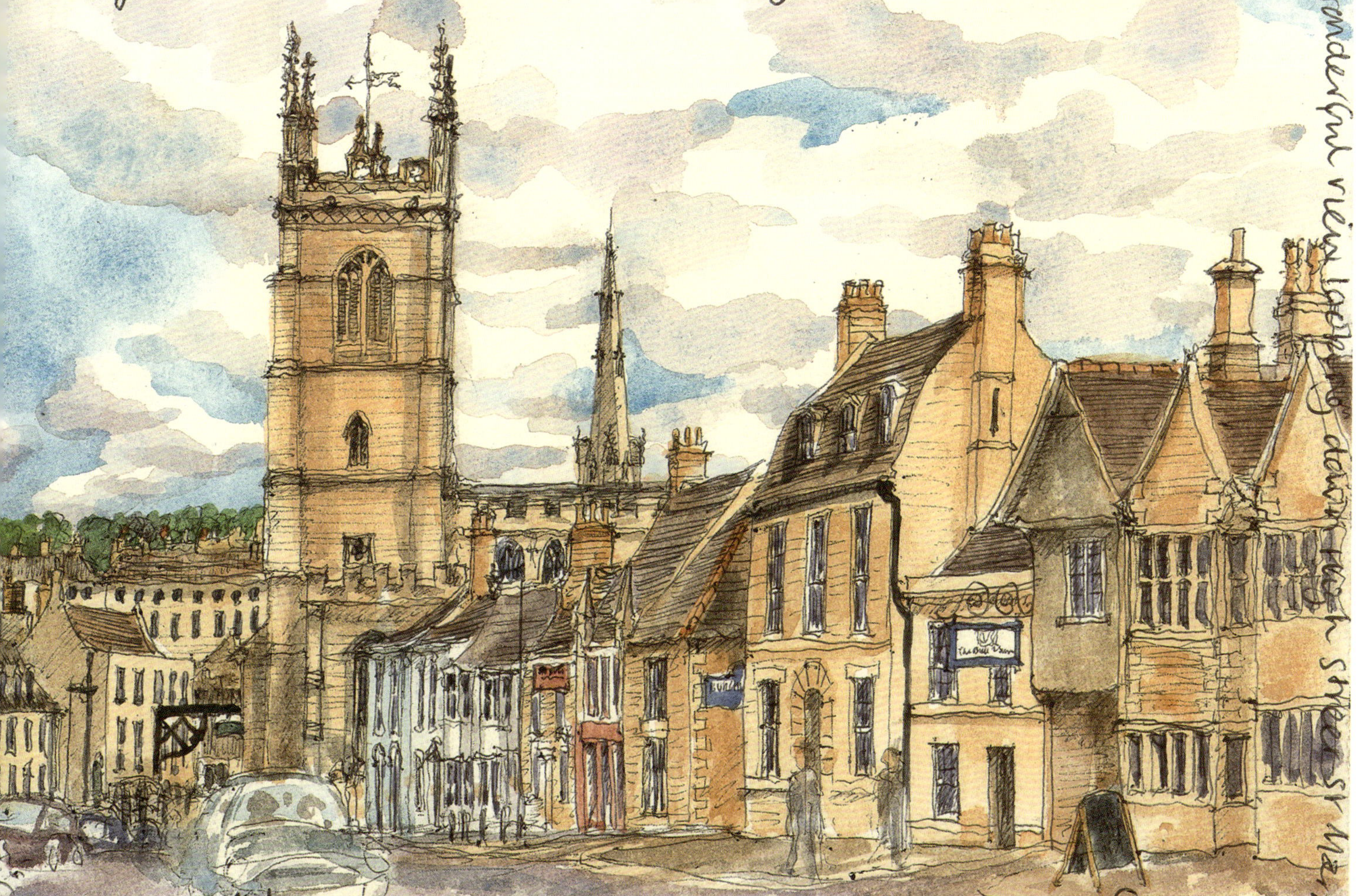

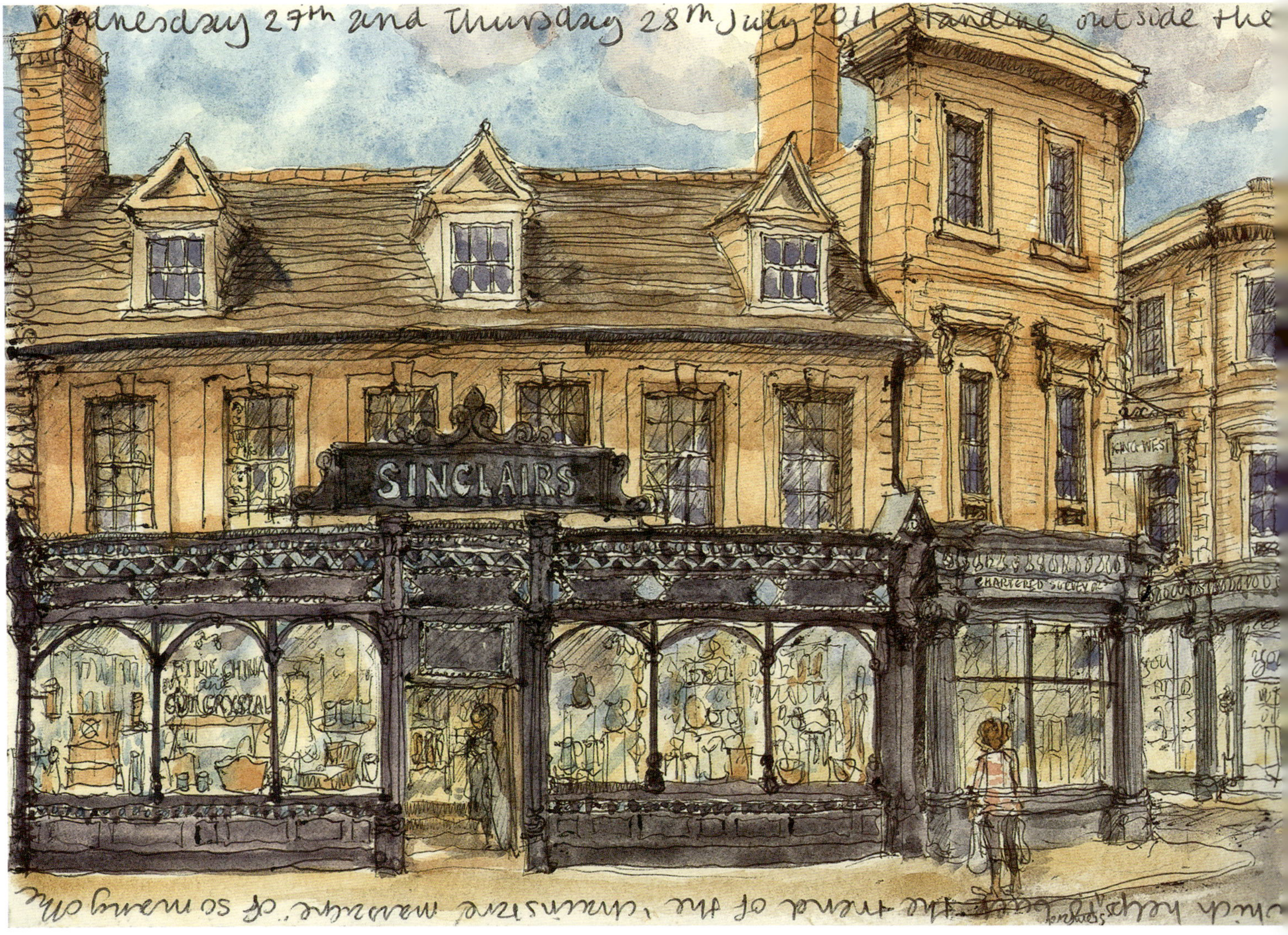
Wednesday 27th and Thursday 28th July 2011. Standing outside the
SINCLAIRS
FINE CHINA and GLASS CRYSTAL
KING WEST
CHARTERED SURVEYORS
the trend of the 'chainstore massacre' of so many othe

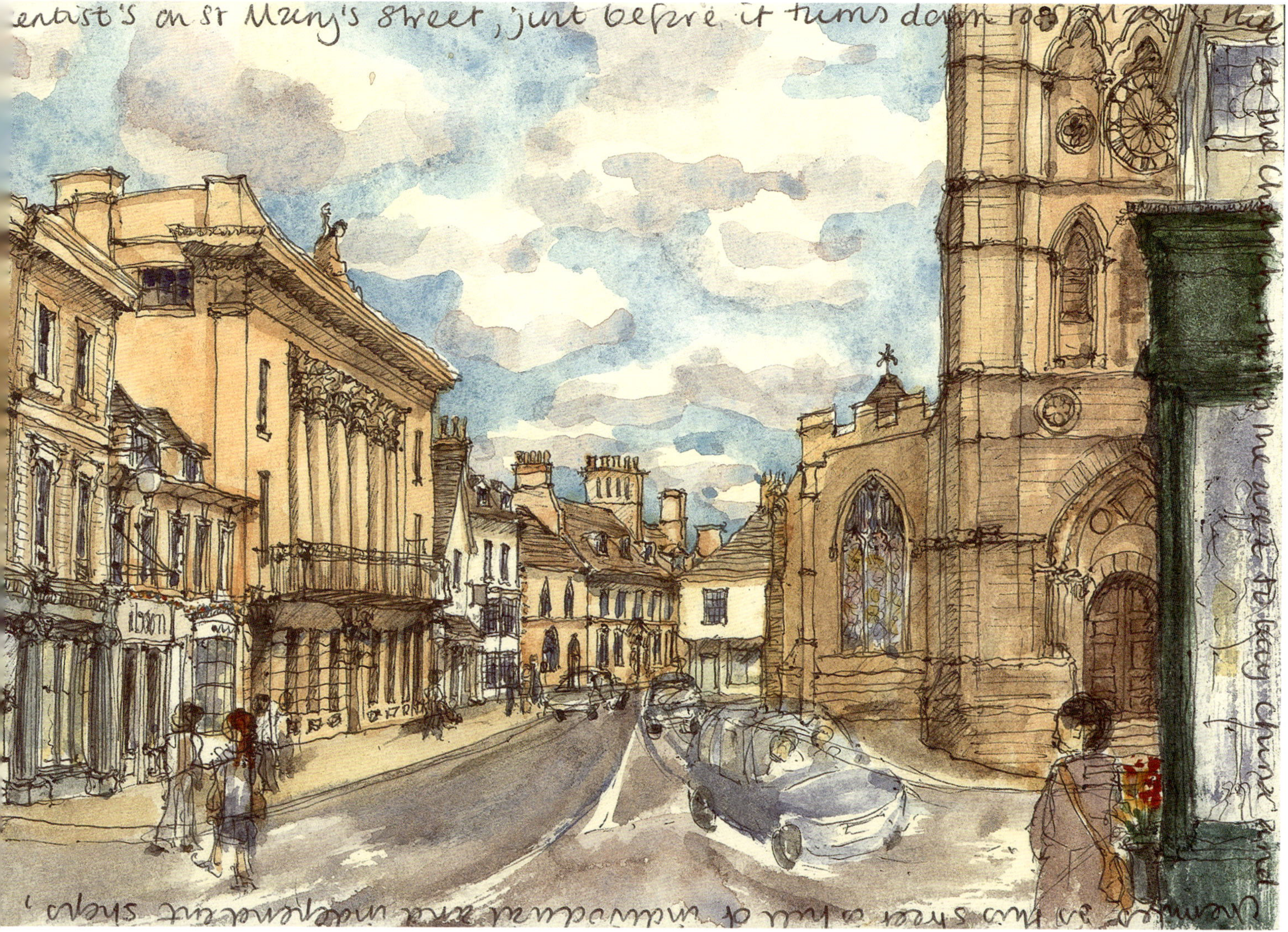
entist's on St Mary's street, just before it turns down

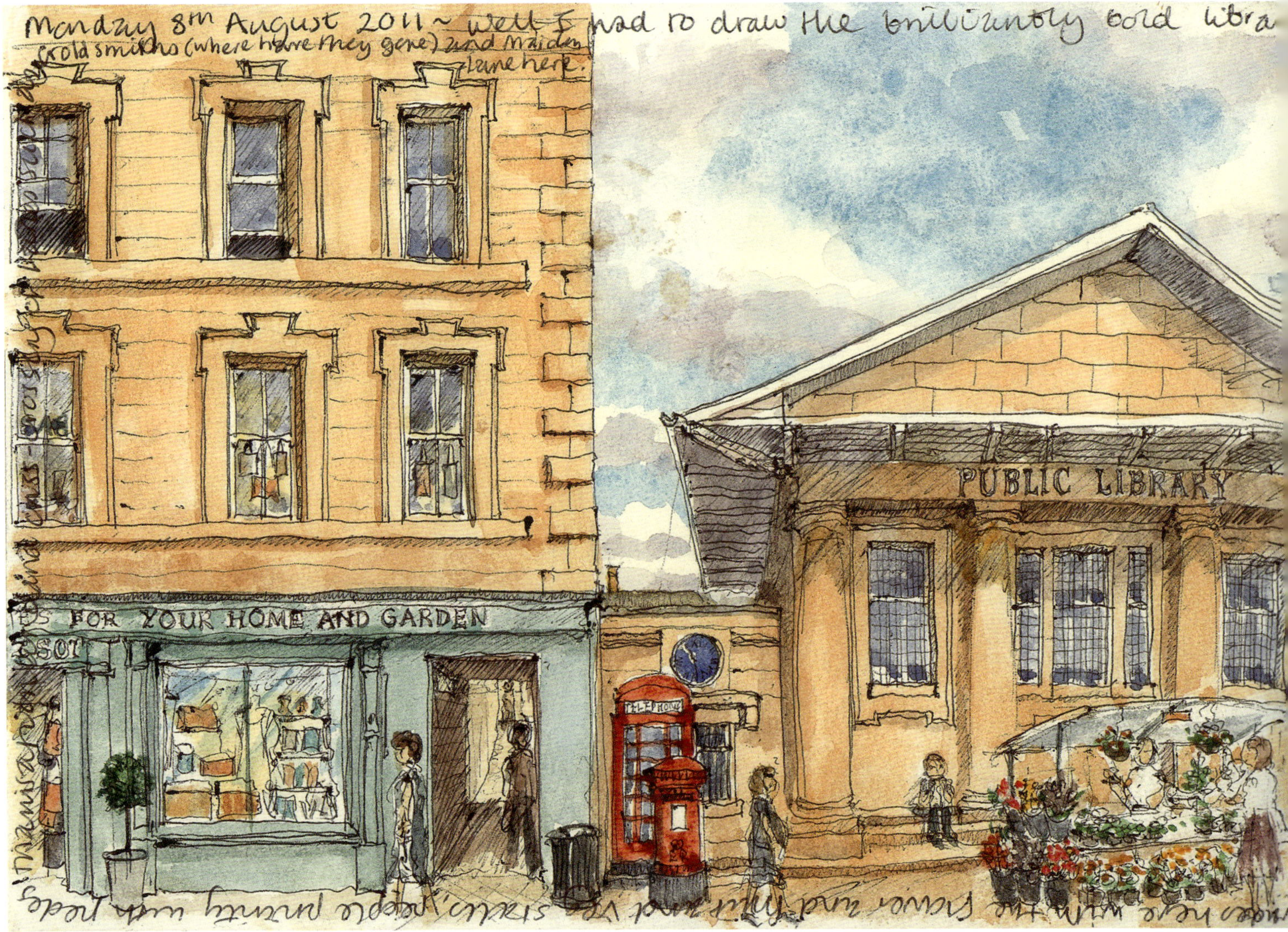

Monday 8th August 2011 ~ well I had to draw the brilliantly bold libra
Goldsmiths (where have they gone) and Maiden lane here.
FOR YOUR HOME AND GARDEN
PUBLIC LIBRARY

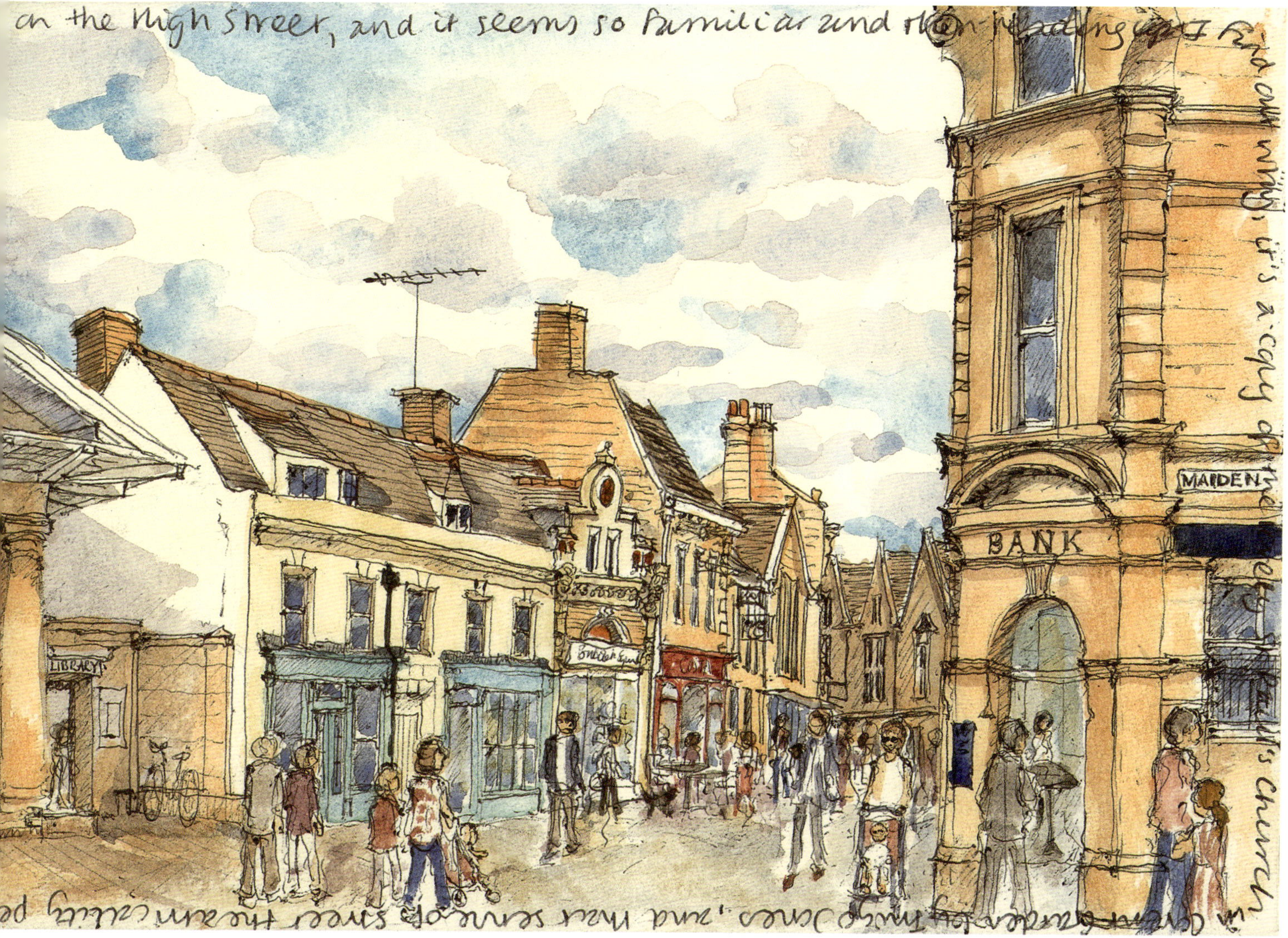
on the High Street, and it seems so familiar and then
find out why; it's a copy of the
Paul's church
LIBRARY
MAIDEN
BANK

## THE TEXT ON THE PAINTINGS

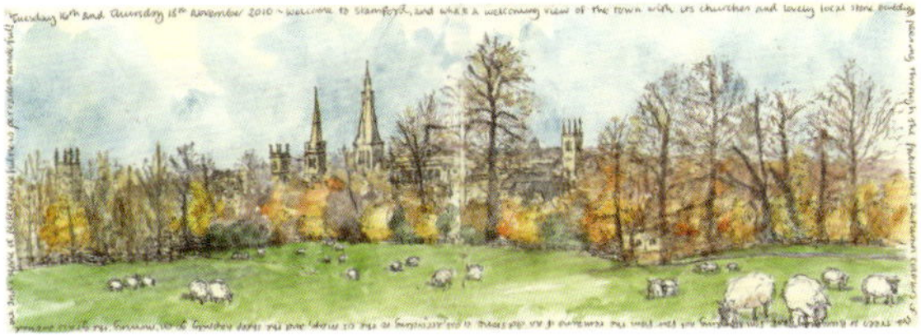

***1*** *- Tuesday 16th and Thursday 18th November 2010*
***Burghley Park looking back to Stamford***
Welcome to Stamford, and what a welcoming view of the town with its churches and lovely local stone buildings peeping through the fabulous autumn colours of the trees at Burghley Park. I'm standing not far from the remains of an old stone cross, according to the OS map, and the sheep happily go on mowing the grass around me and a sense of perfect peacefulness pervades – wonderful!

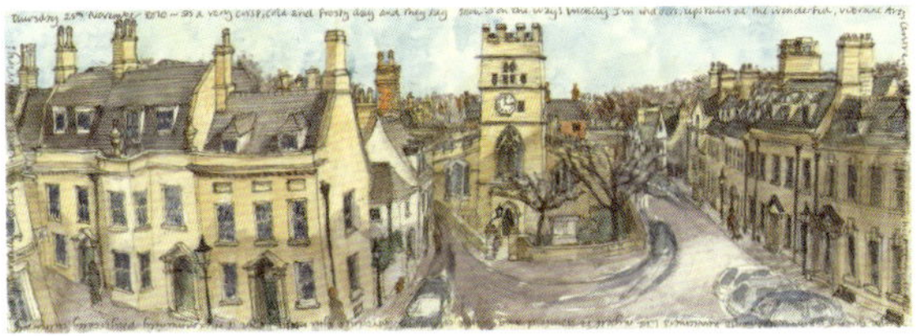

***2*** *- Thursday 25th November 2010*
***St. George's Square from the Arts Centre***
It's a very crisp, cold and frosty morning and they say snow is on the way! Luckily I'm indoors, upstairs at the wonderful, vibrant Arts Centre and just like St. George's, which it overlooks, they've given a warm welcome to newcomers like myself to Stamford, and whose open doors introduce you to the heart of the community physically, culturally and spiritually and it is one which is thriving!

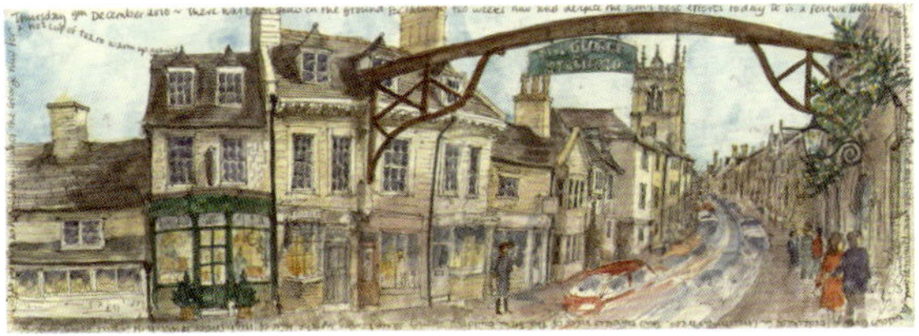

***3*** *- Thursday 9th December 2010*
***Outside the George Hotel***
There has been snow on the ground for almost two weeks now and despite the sun's best efforts today it is a festive frosty frozenness that prevails as I stand outside the famous and fabulous George bedecked in Christmas trees. This timeless view of the stone buildings slowly sauntering up the hill of High Street St. Martin's is just Georgian gorgeousness, as inviting as the window seat of the George now for a hot cup of tea to warm up again!

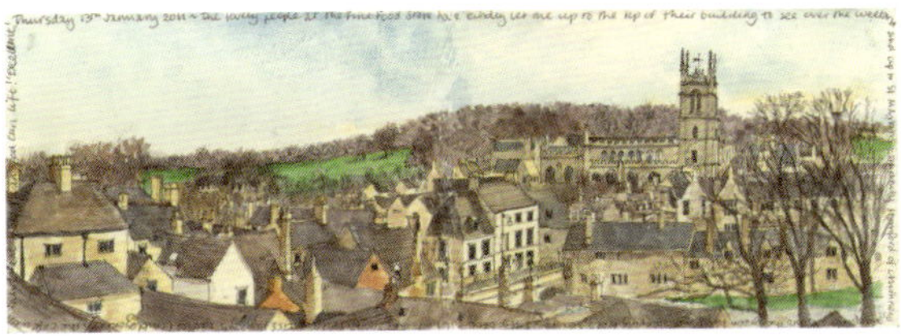

***4*** *- Thursday 13th January 2011*
***View from the top of the Fine Food Store, 37 St. Mary's Street***
The lovely people at the Fine Food Store have kindly let me up to the top of their building to see over the Welland and up to St. Martin's – stunning Stamford of chimneys and spires set into the green hills and sleeping trees, and now I'll go back down to the café to follow Miss Piggy's advice (emblazoned on the café wall) 'Never eat more than you can lift!' Excellent!

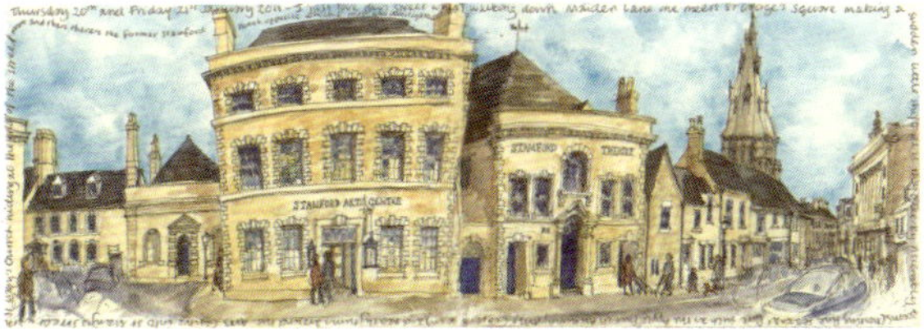

*5 - Thursday 20$^{th}$ and Friday 21$^{st}$ January 2011*
***The Arts Centre and Theatre along St. Mary's Street***
I just love this street, where walking down Maiden Lane one meets St. George's Square making a sudden little shift past the quirky Assembly Rooms (hosting fine seasonal fare such as the Apple Fair in autumn, arts and crafts and so on), and neatly turns around the Arts Centre into St Mary's Street, with St. Mary's Church hiding at the end of the street mmm... and then there's the former Stamford Hotel opposite which I must also investigate......

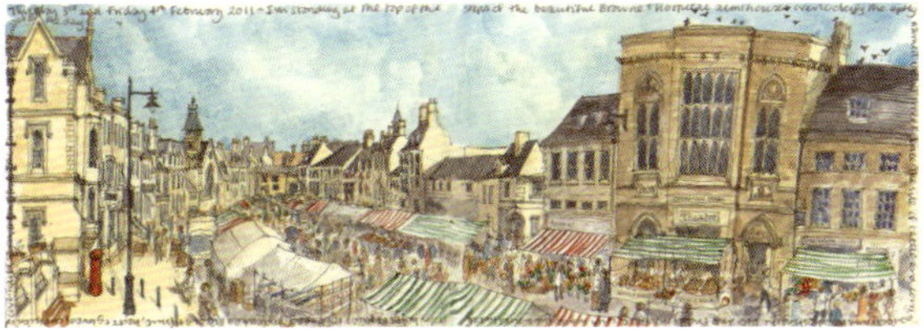

*6 - Thursday 3$^{rd}$ and Friday 4$^{th}$ February 2011*
***Broad Street from the steps of Browne's Hospital on Market Day***
I'm standing at the top of the steps of the beautiful Browne's Hospital almshouses overlooking the aptly named Broad Street, once the site of cattle and corn markets and now hosting the vibrant Friday Market, with wonderful wares for sale from herbs and spices to bread and cakes, flowers and fruits, hats and gloves, cushions and covers and so on. It transforms the street with cars banished for the day.

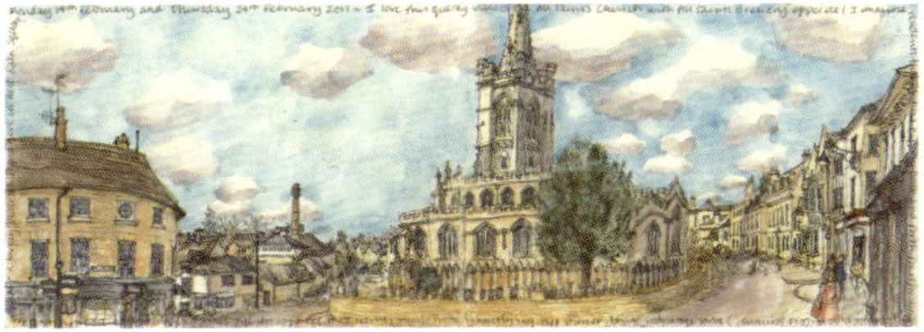

*7 – Monday 14$^{th}$ February and Thursday 24$^{th}$ February 2011*
***Red Lion Square***
I love this quirky view of All Saints church with All Saints Brewery opposite (I imagine residents through time nipping back and forth for refreshment between services and sermons!) and then you sweep around the lovely honey wall of the church and saunter up the sweep of gorgeous, beautiful Barn Hill – a lovely place to stand here in Red Lion Square.

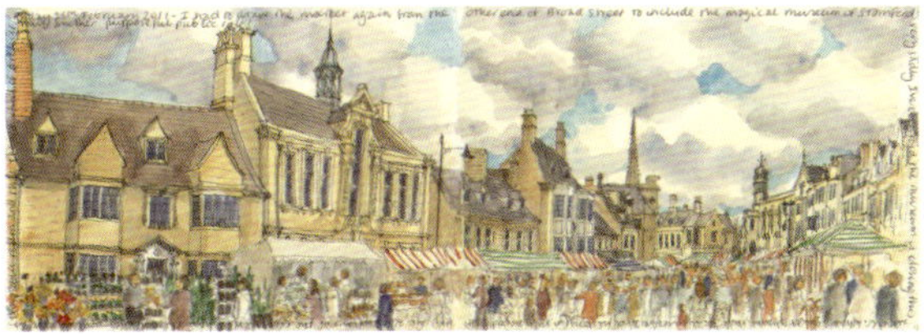

*8 - Friday 25$^{th}$ February 2011*
***Market Day and the Museum, Broad Street***
I had to draw the market again from the other end of Broad Street to include the magical museum of Stamford. Very sadly I've been told that the Museum is closing this summer. What a great shame that local culture and history (in such a good setting) are also victims of the recession. I hope the contents will be kept in the public realm and that the old 'School of Art' will have another purposeful public role!

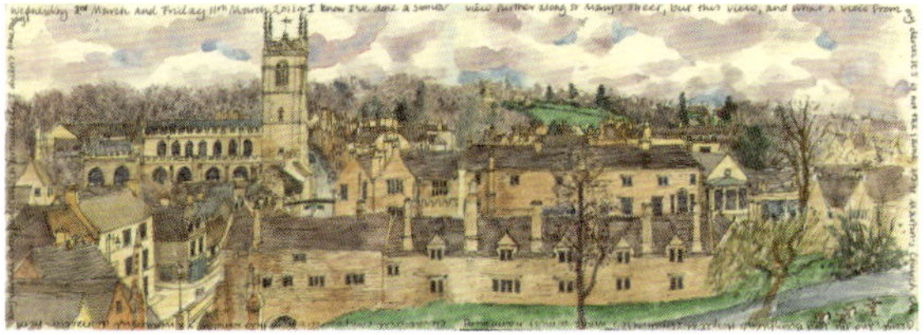

***9** - Wednesday $2^{nd}$ March and Friday $11^{th}$ March 2011*

***View from the Dentist's on St. Mary's Street!***

I know I've done a similar view further along St. Mary's Street, but this view, and what a view, from my dentists is not the same, as St. Martin's Church, the George, and the Lord Burghley's Hospital almshouses make a most harmonious elevational composition from this window – a wonderful distraction from any dental extractions (which fortunately I didn't have today!)

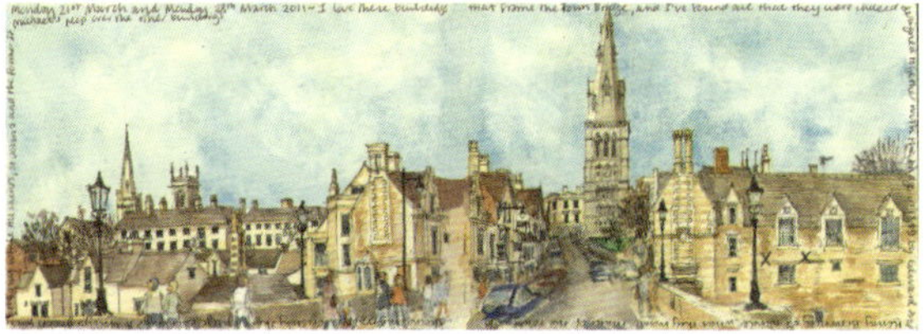

***10** - Monday $21^{st}$ March and Monday $28^{th}$ March 2011*

***View from the Town Bridge***

I love these buildings that frame the Town Bridge, and I've found out that they were indeed designed together with the bridge in 1849 by Edward and Henry Browning. I wonder what they would make of the tonnes of thundering traffic crossing their bridge each day. St. Mary's greets you up the hill while All Saints', St. John's and the former St. Michael's peep over the other buildings.

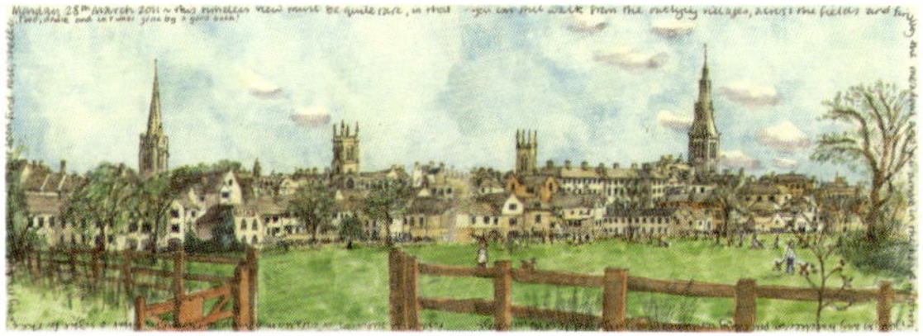

***11** - Monday $28^{th}$ March 2011*

***Stamford from the Meadows***

This timeless view must be quite rare, in that you can still walk from the outlying villages, across the fields and finally the Meadows and you arrive in the heart of town, just as any traveller in preceding centuries – no ring road to cross, or large residential suburbs or estates to navigate through. What a sight for the weary traveller to know that you will soon find rest, shelter, food, drink and in times gone by a good bath!

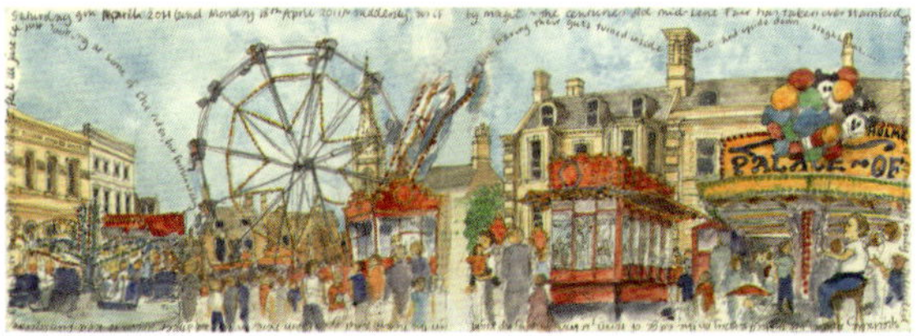

***12** – Saturday $9^{th}$ April 2011(and Monday $18^{th}$ April 2011)*

***The Mid-Lent Fair, Broad Street***

Suddenly as if by magic – the centuries old Mid-Lent Fair has taken over Stamford for the whole first week of April. It is truly a splendid spectacle, as it is not tucked away on the edge of town, it has sprung up right in the heart and goes from here in Broad Street down to Red Lion Square, Bath Row and onto the Meadows. I feel ill just looking at some of the rides, but fortunately the majority of people seem to love having their guts turned inside out and upside down.....aaaghhhh.............

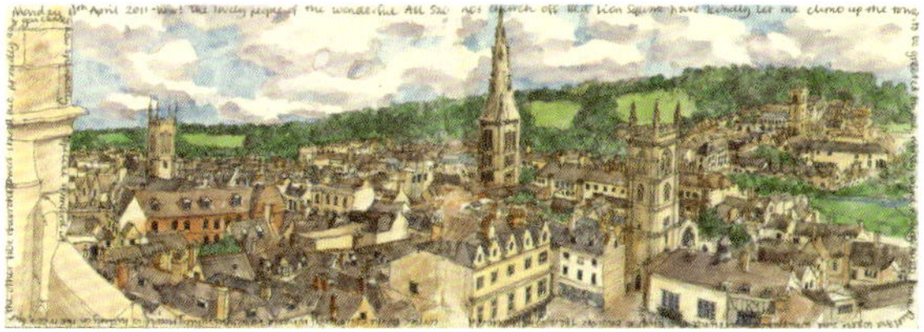

***13** –Monday $11^{th}$ April 2011*
***View from the Top of All Saints' Church***
Wow! The lovely people of the wonderful All Saints' Church off Red Lion Square have kindly let me climb up the tower to be greeted by one windy wind racing across from Rutland Water and whipping up around the tower to ensure there is no sheltered corner for me – but hey what a view! Burghley House is hiding in the trees, but the other five church towers stand out proudly and you can see how splendidly special Stamford is!

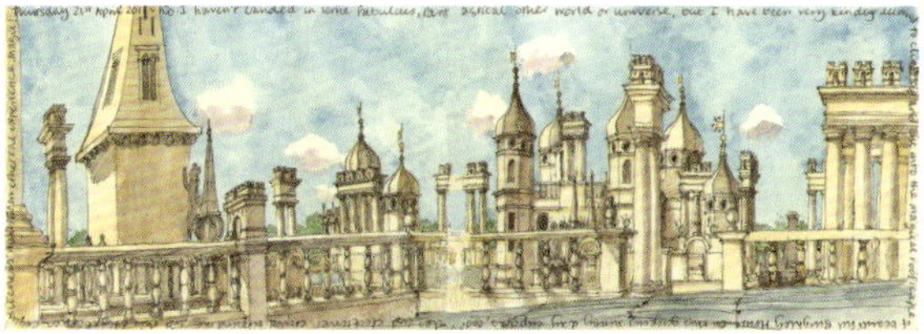

***14** – Thursday $21^{st}$ April 2011*
***The Roof of Burghley House***
No I haven't landed in some fabulous, fantastical other world or universe, but I have been very kindly allowed to climb up and out onto the magical roofscape of beautiful Burghley House. On this gorgeous sunny day, cupolas, castles and clock tower crowd around me and this Elizabethan exquisiteness makes for an ethereal experience. Magic!

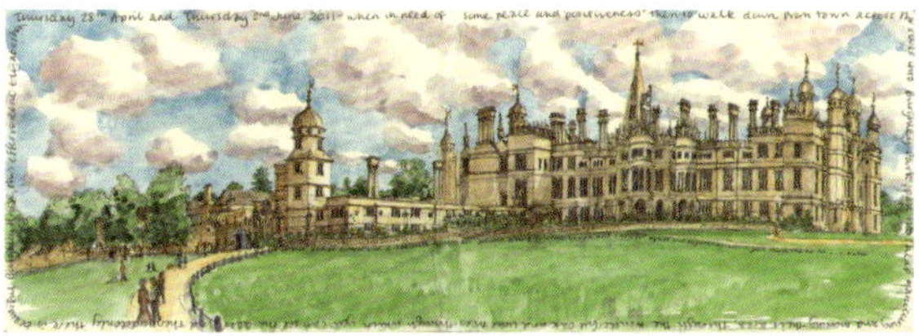

***15** – Thursday $28^{th}$ April and Thursday $2^{nd}$ June 2011*
***Burghley House***
When in need of some peace and 'positiveness', then to walk down from town across the river into Burghley Park, past the sheep manicuring and mowing their area, through the wonderful oak and lime trees, through which you can see the deer and then suddenly there is beautiful Burghley House, this effervescent, Elizabethan edifice, and at either end of the walk you are assured a very welcome cuppa and cake for uplift and rejuvenation.... Just mind the ha-ha.....ha-ha......

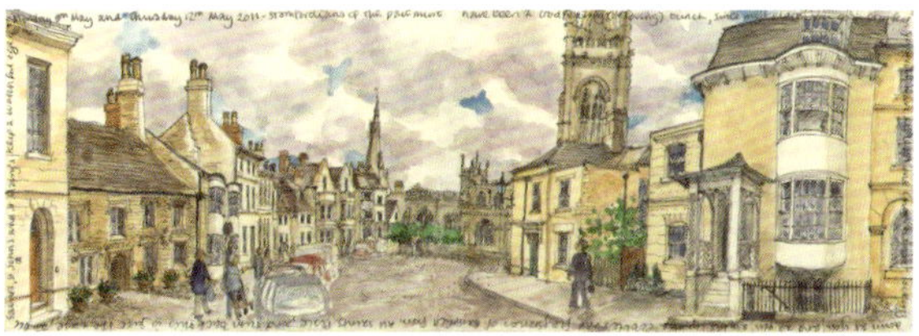

***16** – Monday $9^{th}$ May and Thursday $12^{th}$ May 2011*
***Walking down Barn Hill***
Stamfordians of the past must have been a God fearing (or loving) bunch, since most places you go in Stamford, you will have at least one church tower looking down at you as you amble up the cobbles and flagstones of Barn Hill from All Saints' Place, and turn back this is just the case, as All Saints', St. John's and St. Mary's keep a watchful eye over me!

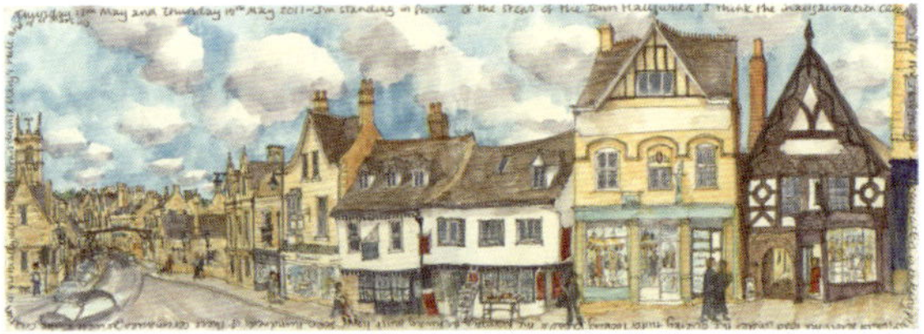

**17** –*Thursday 12th May and Thursday 19th May 2011*
***Outside the Town Hall, St Mary's Hill***
I'm standing in front of the steps of the Town hall where I think the inauguration ceremony for the new mayor and councillors is taking place, whilst across the road, under the quirky Tudor looking facade, the Norman archway must have seen hundreds of these ceremonies, as well as the creation of virtually all of his neighbours down St. Mary's Hill and up St. Martin's......

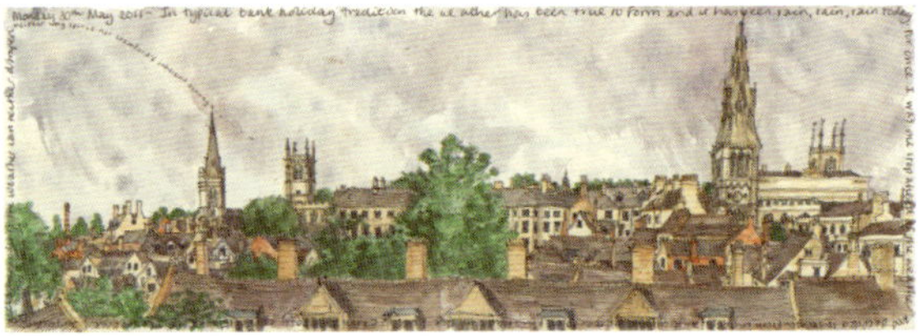

**18** – *Monday 30th May 2011*
***Stamford from a window at the George Hotel, Station Road***
In typical bank holiday tradition the weather has been true to form and it has been rain, rain, rain today. For once I was one step ahead of the weather and decided to sketch from indoors, and where better to do this than in the lovely, calm and cosy environment of the George! In such genteel surroundings the weather can neither dampen my spirit nor Stamford's inherent beauty........

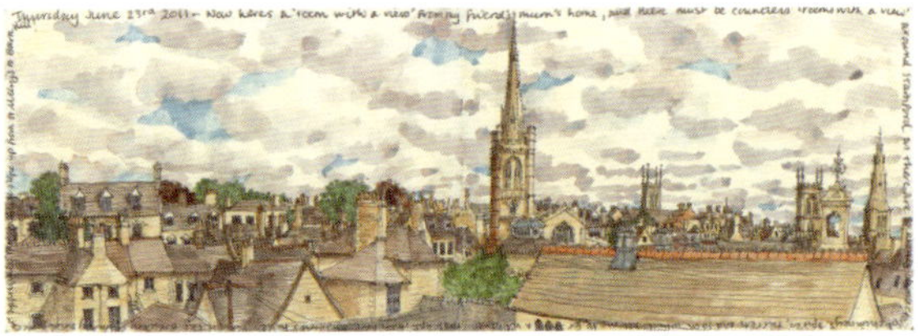

**19** –*Thursday 23rd June 2011*
***Stamford Roofscape, off West Street***
Now here's a 'room with a view' from my friend's mum's home, and there must be countless 'rooms with a view' around Stamford as there are so many characterful chimneys, spires, turrets and so on, which all make for such a vibrant roofscape. From here All Saints' hides behind the Brewery chimney and you can appreciate the gradual slope up from St Mary's to Barn Hill.

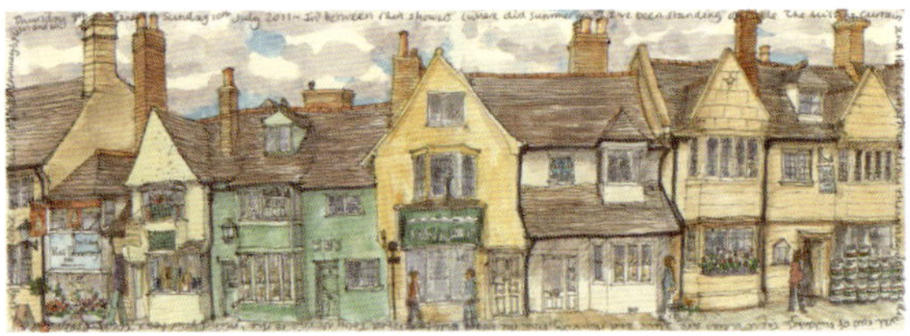

**20** –*Thursday 7th and Sunday 10th July 2011*
***St. Paul's Street***
In between rain showers (where did summer go?) I've been standing outside the Missing Curtain and the car wash to draw this magical medieval row of buildings. These oldies are alive and thriving, from the beautifully restored Toby Norris to the 'mind your head' flower shop and book shop. Welcome to St. Paul's Street, chimneys, gables and all.

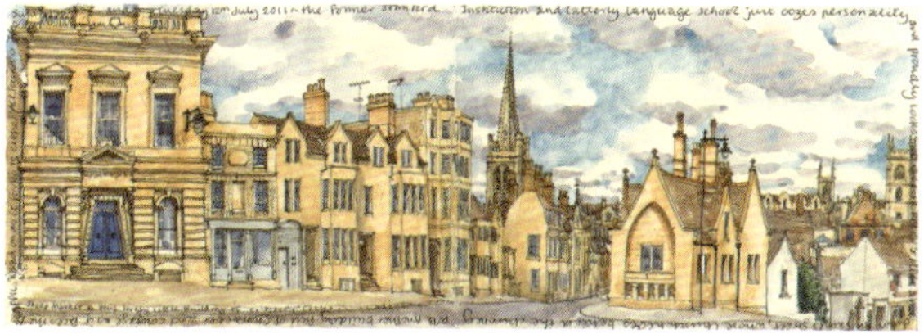

***21** – Sunday 10th and Tuesday 12th July 2011*

***St. Peter's Hill***

The former Stamford Institution and latterly language school just oozes personality and proudly looks out over St. Peter's Hill and down All Saints Street, whose church hides behind the chimney pots. Another building full of character and courage as it faces the traffic head on, as it forks to either All Saints or the Sheep Market is this lovely little building of St. Peter's Callis....... Wheeeee........

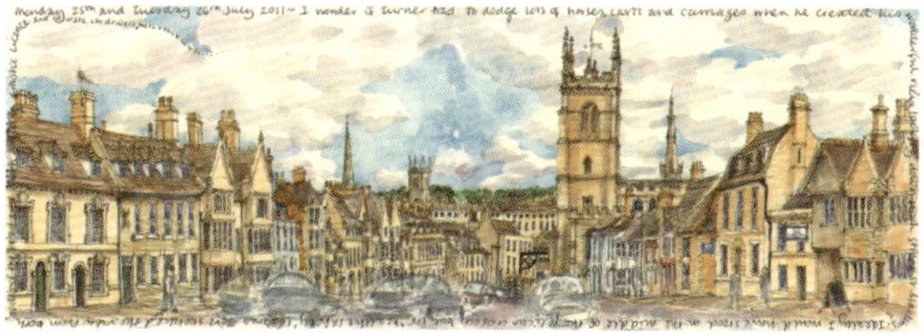

***22** – Monday 25th and Tuesday 26th July 2011*

***High Street St. Martin's***

I wonder if Turner had to dodge lots of horses, carts and carriages when he created his wonderful view looking down High Street St. Martin's. Ideally I would have stood in the middle of the pelican crossing but for 'health and safety' reasons I've sketched the view from both sides of the road and with a little artistic licence and no irate car drivers, here's the view in 2011..........

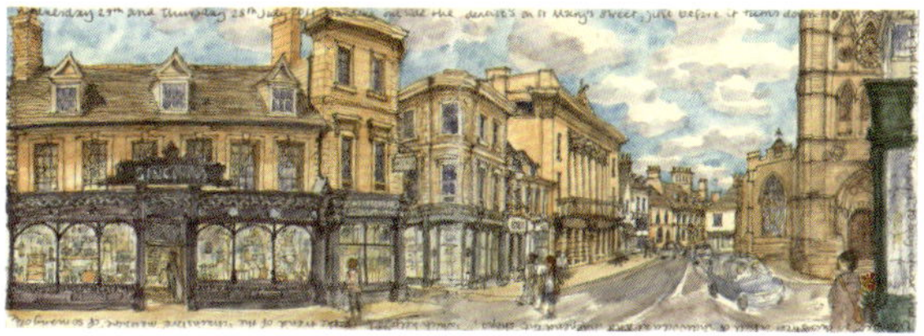

***23** – Wednesday 27th and Thursday 28th July 2011*

***Outside Sinclairs, St. Mary's Street***

Standing outside the dentist's on St. Mary's Street, just before it turns down to St. Mary's Hill at the Church, this is the area to buy china and chemises, as this street is full of individual and independent shops, which helps Stamford buck the trend of the 'chainstore' massacre of so many other towns and is all part of Stamford's 'specialness!'

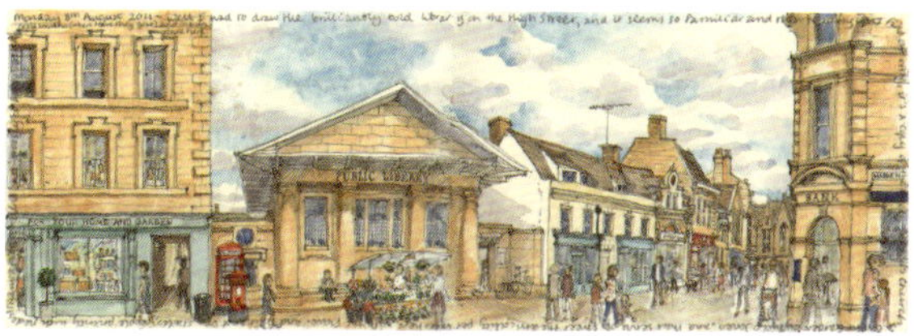

***24** –Monday 8th August 2011*

***The High Street***

Well I had to draw the brilliantly bold library on the High Street, and it seems so familiar, and then reading up I find out why, it's a copy of the lovely St. Paul's Church in Covent Garden by Inigo Jones, and that sense of street theatricality pervades here with the flowers and fruit and veg stalls, people priority with pedestrianisation and criss–crossing of lanes such as Goldsmiths (where have they gone?) and Maiden Lane here.